GROUP
Crisis Support

■

WHY it works
WHEN & HOW
to provide it

Jeffrey T. Mitchell, Ph.D.

Group Crisis Support
Why it works
When and How to provide it

© 2007 Jeffrey T. Mitchell, PhD
Published by Chevron Publishing Corp.
5018 Dorsey Hall Drive, Suite 104
Ellicott City, MD 21042

Cover design by Peggy Johnson
Edited by Diane Gwin
Layout design by Peggy Johnson

Printed in the United States of America.
This book is printed on acid-free paper.

Library of Congress Card Catalog Number
Application in process
ISBN-10: 1-883581-24-9
ISBN-13: 978-1-883581-24-4

CHEVRON
PUBLISHING CORPORATION

5018 Dorsey Hall Drive, Suite 104
Ellicott City, MD 21042 USA
Telephone: (410) 740-0065
Fax: (410) 740-9213
office@chevronpublishing.com

Dedication

To Shannon, my wife, and to my wonderful children, Kyla and Annie: Thank you for all the joy and adventure you bring into my life. Peace and happiness in your every step.

Acknowledgements

It is ironic that writing a book on groups is an isolating experience. It cuts you off from family, friends, and normal life pursuits. I would, first and foremost, acknowledge the huge contributions of my family. Shannon, my wife, and my children, Kyla and Annie, endured seemingly endless hours of my absence as I buried myself in research for this book. They were, however, always there for me and functioned as an integral part of the writing process. They provided encouragement, a listening ear, and a steady supply of homemade cards, drawings, notes, and stickers to encourage me.

Next, Diane Gwin of Chevron Publishing was invaluable as an editor and publisher. I often talked to myself when I read her suggestions and alterations to my writing, and I found myself saying, "Why didn't I say it that way in the first place?" Publishing with a small company like Chevron makes what might be a draining experience under other circumstances, actually become a positive adventure. Diane and her small staff work exceptionally hard to deliver a high quality publication.

I would be remiss if I did not acknowledge the wonderful insights I have gained into traumatic stress and the research field itself from my friend and colleague, George S. Everly, Jr. I have known him for nearly 25 years and I learn from him constantly. Thanks, George.

There are also literally thousands of professional and peer support CISM trained people who deserve a big "thank you" for their inspiration, information, and encouragement. Finally, there are countless firefighters, paramedics, emergency medical technicians, law enforcement, search and rescue, and military personnel who have challenged and encouraged me to do better - always. I appreciate their stories, their accomplishments, their families, whom I have often met, and the immeasurable contributions they make to life.

One of the most genuine compliments I ever received actually represents my feelings toward the many thousands of wonderful people I have met over the years. So, I thought I would pass it on to you. My team and I had just finished a Critical Incident Stress Debriefing after a particularly disturbing event. A firefighter, who was especially quiet during the meeting, gave me a firm slap on the back and said warmly and with a smile as he left the room, "Hey, Doc, that wasn't half bad, Thanks." With a big, sincere smile, I can say the same sort of thing to you. "Folks, what you do for others isn't half bad either, so keep doing it; and do it well!" My very best wishes to all of you.

Jeffrey T. Mitchell, Ph.D.
December 30, 2006

Table of Contents

Constant kindness can accomplish much.
As the sun makes ice melt, kindness
causes misunderstanding,
mistrust, and hostility
to evaporate.

~ Albert Schweitzer

Chapter 1

Crucial Points Before You Begin

"What we call the beginning is often the end. And to make an end is to make a beginning. The end is where we start from"
~ T.S. Eliot *(Playwright, Poet and Critic, 1888-1965)*

INTRODUCTION

There are three essential points that must be perfectly clear before reading further. Failure to understand these primary concepts sets the stage for misinterpretations, misrepresentations, and misapplications of the supportive crisis intervention services for both the large and small groups addressed in this book. Furthermore, a misunderstanding of the issues discussed in this chapter jeopardizes one's comprehension of the entire field of crisis intervention.

Assistance to people in a state of emotional crisis may be labeled with essentially synonymous terms such as, "crisis intervention," "early psychological intervention," "psychological first aid," or "emotional first aid." [1, 2] Regardless of the label applied to crisis support services, reading this book does not substitute for appropriate crisis intervention training. People who lack special training in crisis intervention should not attempt to provide crisis support services. Crisis interventionists should have at least 40 hours of training in skills to manage both cases requiring individual assistance and those requiring crisis intervention services for groups. At a minimum, after training, crisis interventionists should be able to:

- assess the situation and the reactions of the people involved,
- develop a strategic crisis intervention plan,
- be skillful in managing large groups needing information and guidance,
- be skillful in managing small, homogeneous groups through group discussions of traumatic events,
- provide a wide array of follow-up services, and
- make appropriate referrals for those who may need additional support or professional therapy. [3,4,5]

Crucial Points

1. *Group oriented crisis intervention support services must be thought of and applied only* **within the context of a broad program** *or "package" of crisis support services.*

Crisis support services for groups are not stand-alone interventions. To be effective they need to be utilized within a context of a comprehensive, integrated, systematic, and multi-tactic program. The very best outcome results are achieved only when group interventions are used in that manner. Several important recent documents, in fact, suggest a blending of crisis intervention procedures to achieve the maximum positive effects.[4,5,6,7,8] A reasonably comprehensive, although not all inclusive, list of crisis interventions can be found in table 1.1.

Table 1.1

<u>Common Crisis Intervention Services</u>

- Pre-incident planning & training
- Incident assessment and strategic planning
- Acute psychological assessment and triage including facilitation of access to appropriate levels of care when needed
- Psychological first aid
- Crisis intervention with large groups
- Crisis intervention with small groups
- Crisis intervention with individuals (both face-to-face and through hotlines)
- Family crisis intervention
- Spiritual/ Pastoral crisis intervention/ Disaster ministry
- Community crisis planning and intervention
- Organizational crisis planning and intervention
- Post-incident evaluation and training based on lessons learned

2. <u>**Do not**</u> **use the crisis intervention support services for groups** *that are described in this book* **with individual primary victims** *who are ill or injured or who are victims of violence.*

Crisis intervention services that have been designed for groups are not intended for use with individuals. Use supportive, individual crisis intervention processes with individuals. Likewise, when working with groups, choose crisis support services that have been developed specifically for groups. Application of group processes to individuals produces significant distortions in the inherent nature of group processes.[9] Group-oriented crisis intervention procedures should never be applied to individuals who are victims of sexual assault, auto accidents, dog bites, serious burns, or who have experienced miscarriages, difficult pregnancies, post partum depression or other physical or mental maladies. Researchers in several studies have misapplied to individuals processes that were developed for use with groups and the results indicate that such serious mistakes should not be repeated.[10, 11, 12, 13, 14, 15, 16]

3. *The crisis intervention support services for groups described in this book **do not** constitute psychotherapy in any form, nor should they be considered as a substitute for psychotherapy. Additionally, these group support services should not be researched in comparison with psychotherapies or as if they were psychotherapies.*

Attempting to utilize crisis support services for groups as if they were a form of psychotherapy is a dangerous practice. When a person only needs support through a crisis, "psychological first aid" or crisis intervention will usually suffice. If, on the other hand, a person needs psychotherapy and only crisis support services are offered, their psychological condition will not usually improve. In fact, deterioration in psychological status is the more likely outcome.

Do not compare crisis intervention or psychological first aid to psychotherapy. Likewise, crisis intervention should not it be researched as if it were psychotherapy. Comparisons to psychotherapy are unwarranted, unsupported by the literature, and inappropriate. Research about crisis support services for groups should evaluate what the specific group-focused crisis intervention tool was designed to accomplish. The research questions should appraise whether or not a crisis support service for groups provided practical information and mitigated the impact of a traumatic event. Research should assess whether or not group crisis intervention facilitates the recovery processes of normal people who are experiencing normal reactions to abnormal events. Moreover, research in the field of group crisis intervention should determine if those in need of additional support or a referral for professional care are encouraged by the group interventions to seek and accept professional assistance. Keep in mind that crisis intervention is at one end of the spectrum supporting human beings and psychotherapy is at the complete opposite end of that spectrum.

The descriptions and guidelines presented in this book are related to **crisis support services only**. They are **not** clinical prescriptions for the practice of psychiatry, psychology, social work, psychiatric nursing, or mental health counseling of any type. Again, some have attempted these flawed comparisons or have attempted to use crisis intervention as if it were psychotherapy and the results are clearly not positive.[10, 11, 12, 13, 14, 15, 16]

SUMMARY

This chapter clarifies three extremely important points about group crisis interventions. First, they are not to be used to assist groups in crises unless they are applied as components of a more comprehensive, integrated, systematic, and multi-component approach to managing psychological crises. Second, group interventions are not intended to be applied to individuals, especially if those individuals are injured or ill primary victims. Third, group crisis intervention procedures neither are a form of psychotherapy nor are they a substitute for psychotherapy. Do not compare crisis intervention procedures to psychotherapy or research them as if they were a form of psychotherapy.

The three concepts discussed in this chapter are vitally important to the overall understanding of the group procedures described in the remainder of the book. In addition, these principles are essential in understanding the entire field of crisis intervention.

Subsequent chapters will lead the reader through an understanding of crisis and the primary principles of crisis intervention. They will also review the rich history of group crisis intervention before moving on to detailed explorations of the various types of crisis intervention procedures for large and small groups.

REFERENCES - Chapter 1

1. American Psychiatric Association (1964). *First Aid for Psychological Reactions in Disasters*. Washington, DC: American Psychiatric Association.

2. Neil, T., Oney, J., DiFonso, L., Thacker, B., & Reichart, W. (1974). *Emotional First Aid*. Louisville: Kemper-Behavioral Science Associates.

3. Mitchell, J.T. (2003) Major Misconceptions in Crisis Intervention. *International Journal of Emergency Mental Health*, 5 (4), 185-197.

4. National Voluntary Organizations Active in Disasters (2005) Early Psychological Intervention Subcommittee Consensus Points.

5. Mitchell, J.T. (2004). Characteristics of Successful Early Intervention Programs. *International Journal of Emergency Mental Health*, 6 (4), 175-184.

6. Robinson, R. C. & Murdoch, P. (2003). *Establishing and Maintaining Peer Support Program in the Workplace*. Ellicott City, MD: Chevron Publishing Corporation.

7. Richards, D. (2001). A field study of critical incident stress debriefing versus critical incident stress management. *Journal of Mental Health*, 10, 351-362.

8. National Institute of Mental Health. (2002). Mental Health and Mass Violence: Evidence-based early psychological intervention for victims /survivors of Mass violence. A workshop to reach consensus on best practices." Washington, DC: NIMH.

9. Dyregrov, A. (2003). *Psychological Debriefing: A leader's guide for small group* crisis intervention. Ellicott City, MD: Chevron Publishing Corporation.

10. Bisson, J.I., Jenkins, P., Alexander, J., & Bannister, C. (1997). Randomized controlled trial of psychological debriefings for victims of acute burn trauma. *British Journal of Psychiatry*, 171, 78-81.

11. Hobbs, M., Mayou, R., Harrison, B and Worlock, P. (1996). A randomized controlled trial of psychological debriefings of road traffic accidents. *British Medical Journal*, 313, 1438-1439.

12. Rose, S., Brewin, C., Andrews, B and Kirk, M. (1999). A randomized controlled trial of individual psychological debriefing for victims of violent crime. *Psychological Medicine*, 29, 793-799.

13. Rose, S., Bisson, J., & Wessely, S. (2002). Psychological debriefing for preventing post traumatic stress disorder (PTSD). *The Cochrane Library*, Issue 1. Oxford, UK: Update Software.

14. van Emmerik, A.A.P., Kamphuis, J.H., Hulsbosch, A.M., & Emmelkamp, P.M.G (2002). Single session debriefing after psychological trauma: a meta-analysis. *Lancet*, 360, 766-771.

15. Wessely, S., Rose, S., & Bisson, J. (1998). A systematic review of brief psychological interventions (debriefing) for the treatment of immediate trauma related symptoms and the prevention of post traumatic stress disorder (Cochrane Review). *Cochrane Library*, Issue 3, Oxford, UK: Update Software.

16. Lee, C., Slade, P., and Lygo, V (1996). The influence of psychological debriefing on emotional adaptation in women following early miscarriage. *British Journal of* Medical Psychology, 69, 47-58.

Chapter 2

Crisis and Crisis Intervention

"Prophylactically, it is probable that many disorders could be nipped in the bud if prompt attention could be given...
First aid treatment by its very nature should be very flexible and expedient, utilizing every possible method of achieving results...
...Psychological first aid must utilize many of the older orthodox methods which ... operate primarily only upon symptomatic levels. Reassurance is probably the first aid method par excellence ... Suggestion can be used to deal with acute symptoms requiring immediate attention. Catharsis may be mind-saving for people bursting over with acute tensions.
Persuasion, advice and other supportive methods may help the client to deal with acute situational problems which are beyond his resources."
~ F.C.T. - Editorial on Psychological First Aid, Journal of Clinical Psychology, April, 1952, 8(2), pp. 210-211.

INTRODUCTION

We live in a world that is, on one hand, good, beautiful, awe inspiring, and filled with human gentleness, sympathy, and kindness. On the other hand, that very same world is also filled with evil, pain, loss, destruction, selfishness, cruelty, terror, and horror. Individuals struggle to adapt to and to deal with the fortunes and misfortunes of life on earth. The turmoil produced by the negative aspects of life may leave a person shaken and extremely distressed. It is then that they may seek crisis intervention assistance, support, and guidance from others.

Sometimes entire groups or even communities and nations are overwhelmed by small, common tragedies or by huge catastrophes beyond human comprehension. Such was the experience of many in the aftermath of the brutal attacks of September 11, 2001. Large, diverse groups of commuters from other states as well as local businessmen and women were seriously stressed. So were homogeneous groups of frightened people from schools, churches, and community organizations. Small companies of firefighters and units of police officers, who lost colleagues but continued to function with exceptional valor and selflessness, were also in need of support. Many types of groups were impacted and overwhelmed by the shock of the attacks.

This book, however, is not specifically related to disasters or, for that matter, large-scale events. Instead, it has been written for people who are in the position of trying to help groups or communities make sense out of either everyday crisis events or the chaos of a major disaster. It is a group crisis intervention guidebook. The book's focus is on common sense crisis intervention and stress management techniques. The crisis intervention support services for large and small groups detailed in this book have a long history of successful applications to many different types of groups under many different circumstances.

This chapter will cover the key terms of crisis intervention before briefly reviewing its history. It will conclude with the principles and guidelines of effective crisis intervention.

SOME KEY TERMS

The most logical place to start to develop an understanding of the key terms associated with crisis and crisis intervention is the term, *critical incident*. Many of the other crisis terms are directly related to this term.

Critical Incidents

Critical incidents are traumatic events that cause powerful emotional reactions in people who are exposed to them. Disasters and terrorist attacks are among the most distressing for individuals, groups, and communities, but they are not the only critical incidents. Every profession can list their own worst-case scenarios that can be categorized as *critical incidents*. Emergency services organizations, for example, usually list the "Terrible Ten" as critical incidents. They are:

- Line of duty deaths
- Suicide of a colleague
- Serious work related injury
- Multi-casualty, disaster, and terrorism incidents
- Events with a high degree of threat to the personnel
- Significant events involving children
- Events in which the victim is known to the personnel
- Events with excessive media interest

- Events that are prolonged and end with a negative outcome
- Any significantly powerful, overwhelming distressing event

The critical incident occurs first and the crisis reaction follows. Without critical incidents, there would be no crisis reactions and no need for crisis intervention services.[1]

Crisis

A crisis is an acute emotional reaction to a powerful stimulus or demand (the critical incident). A crisis is also known as a state of emotional turmoil. A crisis reaction can further be thought of as an internal, subjective reaction to any significant, powerful experience that impairs a person's ability to think clearly, to cope with distress, or to take actions in their own best interests.

There are two main types of crises. The first is **maturational crisis**. Maturational crises are those that come about as a result of development, experience, growth, or aging as a human being. Retirement, for example, may be a crisis for some people because they must shift from the intense activity of daily work to a completely new set of interests and pursuits.

The second type of crisis is a **situational crisis**. This crisis reaction is caused by exposure to some extremely demanding or overwhelming critical incident such as an accident, an injury, an act of violence, a severe threat, the death of a loved one, or a sudden illness.

There are three characteristics of all crises: 1) the usual balance between thinking and emotions is disturbed. Thinking tends to become less prominent as the emotions become excessive. 2) The usual coping mechanisms that always worked in the past now fail. 3) There is evidence of significant distress, impairment, or dysfunction in the individual or in an entire group involved in the critical incident.[2, 3, 4]

Critical Incident Stress (CIS)

Critical Incident Stress is a state of cognitive, physical, emotional, and behavioral arousal that accompanies the crisis reaction. The elevated state of arousal is caused by a distressing critical incident. If not managed and resolved appropriately, either by oneself or with assistance, CIS may lead to several psychological disorders, including but not limited to the following:

- Acute Stress Disorder
- Panic Disorder

- "panic attacks"
- major clinical depression
- extreme fear (phobic) reactions
- dissociation (out of body or "as if in a movie") reactions
- brief psychotic reactions
- stress related physical disease
- some personality disorders
- abuse of alcohol and other drugs
- Posttraumatic Stress Disorder (PTSD)[1, 5, 6, 7]

Crisis Intervention

Crisis intervention is an active, temporary, and supportive process for individuals or groups who are experiencing an acute state of emotional distress. Crisis intervention may also be referred to as "emotional first aid" or "psychological first aid" or "early psychological intervention." In this book, the term *crisis intervention* will be the term used most often. Crisis intervention has been developed over the last century as an organized and systematic approach, designed to assist a distressed person or a group to return to adaptive function and to recover from the crisis reaction.

The tools used in crisis interventions for individuals, however, are different than those that are used in crisis intervention for groups. The needs, issues, and concerns of individuals are not the same as those for groups. Groups can be very different from individuals. Different types of interventions are therefore necessary.

Critical Incident Stress Management

Critical Incident Stress Management (CISM) is a comprehensive, integrated, systematic, and multi-component "package" of crisis intervention tools (See table 2.1). Some of those tools are used to support individuals in a state of crisis. Other tools are used to assist large or small groups, and some are used to assist families and organizations. The combination of and interrelationship between CISM tools adds to their strength and effectiveness. In other words, no single intervention, used as a stand-alone technique, is as effective as a combination of crisis intervention procedures. As intended by the original design, each crisis intervention tool must be linked to and interwoven with other crisis intervention processes.[7, 8]

Table 2.1

The Meanings of CISM

C =	Critical		C	= Comprehensive
I =	Incident		I	= Integrated
S =	Stress		S	= Systematic
M =	Management		M	= Multi-component

A Brief History of Crisis Intervention

The field of crisis intervention, which, as stated previously, may also be referred to as emotional first aid[9] or psychological first aid,[10] reached a major landmark in the year 2006. That year marked the 100th anniversary of the entry of crisis intervention into formal psychological practices and subsequently into the psychological literature. Edwin Stierlin was the first to write an article on the crisis intervention procedures used in a 1906 European mining disaster.[11] In the United States, in the same year, the National Save-a-Life League was founded in New York in an effort to prevent suicides.[12]

In World War I, Dr. Thomas Salmon applied crisis intervention tactics with combat troops and discovered substantial positive effects.[13] Eric Lindemann and others expanded crisis intervention concepts and applied them to disasters and grief situations.[14,15] Gerald Caplan developed most of the theoretical foundations and basic principles of crisis intervention as we know them today.[2,3,4] It was Caplan who suggested that family members, friends, colleagues, and paraprofessionals could provide the best emotional first aid or psychological first aid.

By the 1950s crisis intervention-based suicide prevention programs were being developed.[16, 17] In 1963, President John F. Kennedy called for a "bold new approach" to the delivery of mental health services. A short time later, the National Community Mental Health Centers' Act was passed by Congress. A network of community mental health centers was developed and a major emphasis was placed on crisis intervention services as a form of preventive outreach.[12]

Crisis intervention procedures gradually expanded from an almost total focus on individuals in the early 1900s to a variety of innovative group support services during World War II. Later, by the mid 1970s, specific group intervention models were developed. Group crisis intervention services with emergency personnel were instituted in 1974. This was widely considered an innovative advance in the field of crisis intervention.[18]

During the last 100 years, four major influences on the development of crisis intervention theory and practice can be identified. They are:

- Warfare
- Disasters/terrorism
- Developments in law enforcement psychological support
- Developments in emergency medical services and firefighting staff support.[1, 19-27]

Today, crisis intervention services are utilized in military and emergency services, in businesses and industries, in schools, hospitals, churches, community organizations, and within governmental agencies.[28] If all the services provided by crisis intervention programs were combined into a summary statistic, almost 40 million crisis intervention contacts would be made in an average year.[29] In just a hundred years time, crisis intervention services became a formal component of psychology and are now interwoven in some fashion with most human endeavors.[30]

Principles of Crisis Intervention

The crisis intervention experience of the last 100 years has generated seven basic principles that guide us in the provision of psychological first aid.

The very first principle is to provide support services close to the person's or group's familiar surroundings, as long as the environment is in a reasonably safe zone. This is the principle of **proximity**.[13]

The second principle is **immediacy,** meaning that help must come quickly. The longer crisis intervention services are delayed, the less effective those interventions will be.[31]

People in a state of crisis are vulnerable to help or further hurt. They are also more open to suggestions than at most other times of their lives. The third principle is based on this openness; it is the principle of **expectancy**. This means that if the helper suggests a positive response to the crisis, it is more likely to come about. On the other hand, if the helper suggests a negative outcome then that will more likely to be the result. It is better to say, "I know the situation you are in now is quite painful. Past experience, however, indicates that most people do recover and return to their normal life activities." In the early stages of a crisis the person providing help should instill hope that it is possible to manage and resolve the situation.[13, 20, 32] The fourth principle of crisis intervention is **brevity**. No one has the luxury of abundant time in a crisis and the capacity to concentrate for most people is substantially reduced. Crisis support services, therefore, must be brief.[15]

The fifth principle is **simplicity**. People have a difficult time handling complex problem solving when they are in the midst of a crisis reaction. Crisis intervention suggestions, therefore, must be easily applied. Simple, well thought out interventions have the greatest potential to be helpful in the majority of cases.

Crises present unusual and often new challenges. Support personnel will not find directions for managing every crisis written down somewhere. Many situations demand that a person helping in a crisis employ **innovation**. The ability to be innovative is the sixth essential principle of crisis intervention.

Finally, whatever actions are chosen in a crisis should be in accordance with the principle of **practicality**. Impractical solutions are no solutions at all. People struggling through a painful experience will see them as insensitive and uncaring.

Table 2.2 lists the seven core principles of all crisis intervention services, whether they be individually focused or oriented toward group support services. Anyone who provides crisis intervention should always have the core principles in mind and should make every effort to incorporate them into the work they do to benefit others.

Table 2.2

The Seven Core Principles of Crisis Intervention

1. Proximity

2. Immediacy

3. Expectancy

4. Brevity

5. Simplicity

6. Innovation

7. Practicality

(2- 4, 9, 12, 14, 18, 19, 29, 31, 32, 33, 34, 35)

There are several other important crisis intervention principles that can help you to assist others. The first is: *stay within your training levels*. Never do things in crisis work unless you have been properly trained. Call in assistance or make a referral if you lack appropriate training and experience for a specific crisis intervention task.

Always take care of the physical safety, and security needs of a person before anything else. Handling the immediate needs of a person in distress is the primary step in all crisis intervention. In fact, it is the most obvious form of psychological or emotional first aid. Failure to acknowledge and relieve physical, safety, information, and security pressures sets the stage for a failure of the overall crisis intervention process.

Crisis support personnel should *avoid "opening up" any topic that cannot be "shut down" in the time available* to work with the person experiencing the crisis. Do not get into deep and complex discussions if there is insufficient time to hear everything in its entirety. Cutting someone off when they have not finished their story is very distressing. Avoid it!

Crisis intervention may have therapeutic elements but it does not constitute psychotherapy nor should it be considered as a substitute for psychotherapy. Crisis intervention cannot be used to manage deep-seated psychological problems. One cannot achieve substantial, long-lasting life changes in the midst of a crisis. Keep your expectations reasonable.

Do not encourage discussions of excessive details of old psychological material when dealing with a crisis. Focus on the "here and now" issues. Do not explore excessive details about past situations or psychological problems. If you encounter someone who obviously needs psychotherapy, make a referral to a mental health professional.[36, 37]

If signs of improvement do not appear after three to five brief crisis intervention contacts, consideration should be given to a referral for additional care. Crisis intervention should only last long enough to be helpful. Make a referral immediately if the distress is extreme, if no calming or recovery is evident, or if serious impairment persists beyond the first three contacts.

Table 2.3 offers some guidance on the number of contacts that are typical in crisis intervention and the number of contacts that indicate a need for a referral.

Objectives of Crisis Intervention

Keep the primary objectives of crisis intervention in mind. Crisis intervention is helpful, but there are substantial limitations. Do not establish outcome expectations that are far beyond its capabilities. Crisis intervention cannot cure physical diseases or significant mental disturbance. It is **not** a cure for Posttraumatic Stress Disorder or other conditions caused by an exposure to a traumatic experience. The primary objectives for crisis intervention are

- stabilization of the situation and mitigation of the impact of a critical incident or traumatic event,
- sacilitation of recovery processes by mobilizing the person's resources,
- normalization ("de-medicalization") of the crisis reactions
- restoration to adaptive function,
- identification of individuals who may need additional support or a referral for psychotherapy. [1, 38, 39]

Table 2.3

General Contact Guidelines for Crisis Intervention

3 to 5 brief contacts are typical (e.g. any combination of individual crisis intervention, small group support services and individual follow-up contacts including telephone support or brief visits).

6 or 7 contacts may be necessary in some cases. If no progress has been made by the 5th contact, a referral for professional care becomes more likely. Referral for professional care should be seriously considered after 5 contacts.

8 or more crisis intervention contacts - Professional referral is indicated.

Critical Incident Stress Management (CISM) should be thought of only as a subset of the field of crisis intervention. A *subset* is defined as a collection of elements within a certain category that are clearly related to each other and all of which can be found within a larger "umbrella" category. Every aspect of the subset, CISM, can be found within the main category, crisis intervention. No matter how many elements a CISM program contains (individual support, family services, large group and small group interventions, follow-up service, pre-incident education, etc.) they are all aspects of crisis intervention. They, therefore, share the same history, theoretical foundations, principles, goals, strategies, procedures, methods, and techniques associated with crisis intervention.[40]

The principles of crisis intervention described in the previous section are in effect whenever the term Critical Incident Stress Management (CISM) is used within this book.

Tactics for Crisis Intervention and Stress Control

No single crisis intervention or stress control technique will be equally applicable to all people, under all circumstances, and at all times. Similar to having a toolbox filled with many different tools, we must have a collection of crisis intervention or stress control techniques that can be utilized for different people under different circumstances. When we pick the right crisis intervention "tool" for the job, the task will be easier and we will have a far better chance of achieving the goals of crisis intervention.

SUMMARY

This chapter provides an overview of the issues of critical incidents, crisis reactions, crisis intervention or "psychological first aid", and the comprehensive, integrated, systematic, and multi-component package of crisis intervention techniques called "Critical Incident Stress Management." The beginning segments of the chapter define and describe core terms and concepts in crisis intervention. Later segments offer a brief review of the history of crisis intervention and provide the basic principles of crisis intervention. Primary objectives of crisis intervention are presented before the chapter concludes with recommendations for a broad spectrum of crisis intervention tactics.

Basic crisis intervention concepts and specific suggestions regarding crisis intervention tactics would be difficult to overemphasize. Everything we do in group-oriented crisis intervention is enormously dependant on a clear working knowledge of the nature of crises as well as the supportive intervention measures that have been developed over the last century.

The next chapter puts crisis intervention on a continuum of care. The most sensible and most effective approach to crisis intervention is a strategic approach. When the many tactics within the field of crisis intervention are applied in a strategic manner, the right interventions can be matched to the circumstances and to the needs of those involved. A strategic approach helps us to apply the support services at the best time, under the right conditions, and by the most appropriate resources.

REFERENCES - Chapter 2

1. Mitchell, J.T. & Everly, G.S., Jr., (2001). *Critical Incident Stress Debriefing: An* operations manual for CISD, Defusing and other group crisis intervention *services, Third Edition.* Ellicott City, MD: Chevron.

2. Caplan, G. (1961). *An approach to Community Mental Health.* New York: Grune and Stratton

3. Caplan, G. (1964). *Principles of Preventive Psychiatry.* New York: Basic Books.

4. Caplan, G. (1969). Opportunities for school psychologists in the primary prevention of mental health disorders in children, In A. Bindman and A. Spiegel (Eds.) *Perspectives in Community Mental Health* (pp.420-436). Chicago: Aldine.

5. Antonellis, P.J.and Mitchell, S.G. (2005). *Posttraumatic Stress Disorder in Firefighters: The calls that stick with you.* Ellicott City, MD: Chevron Publishing Corporation.

6. Everly, G.S. and Lating, J.M. (2004). *Personality-guided therapy for post-traumatic stress disorder.* Washington, DC: American Psychological Association.

7. Everly, G.S., Jr. & Mitchell, J.T. (1999). *Critical Incident Stress Management: A new era and standard of care in crisis intervention.* Ellicott City, MD: Chevron Publishing Corp.

8. Everly, G.S.& Mitchell, J.T. (2002). *Critical Incident Stress Management: Crisis intervention, A workbook, 2ⁿᵈ edition (revised).* Ellicott City, MD: International Critical Incident Stress Foundation.

9. Neil, T., Oney, J., DiFonso, L., Thacker, B., & Reichart, W. (1974). *Emotional First Aid.* Louisville: Kemper-Behavioral Science Associates.

10. American Psychiatric Association (1964). *First Aid for Psychological Reactions in Disasters.* Washington, DC: American Psychiatric Association.

11. Stierlin, E. (1909) *Psycho-neuropathology as a result of a Mining Disaster March 10, 1906.* Zurich: University of Zurich.

12. Roberts, A. (2005). Bridging the Past and Present to the Future of Crisis Intervention and Crisis Management. In Allen Roberts (Ed.) *Crisis Intervention Handbook:Assessment, Treatment and Research. Third Edition.* New York: Oxford University Press.

13. Salmon, T.S. (1919). War neuroses and their lesson. *New York Medical Journal,* 108, 993-994.

14. Lindemann, E. (1944). Symptomatology and management of acute grief. *American Journal of Psychiatry,* 101, 141-148.

15. Parad, L. and Parad, H. (1968). A study of crisis oriented planned short – term treatment: Part II. *Social Casework,* 49, 418-426.

16. Shneidman, E. & Farberow, N. (1957). *Clues to Suicide.* New York: McGraw-Hill.

17. Farberow, N.L. and Shneidman, E. (Eds.) (1965). *The Cry for Help.* New York: McGraw Hill.

18. Everly, G.S., Jr. (1999). Emergency Mental Health: An Overview. *International Journal of Emergency Mental Health,* 1, 3-7.

19. Artiss, K. (1963). Human behavior under stress: From combat to social psychiatry. *Military Medicine,* 128, 1011-1015.

20. Solomon, Z. and Benbenishty, R. (1986). The role of proximity, immediacy, and expectancy in frontline treatment of combat stress reaction among Israelis in the Lebanon War. *American Journal of Psychiatry,* 143, 613-617.

21. North, C.S. & Pfefferbaum, B. (2002). Research on the mental Health Effects of Terrorism. *JAMA,* 288 (5), 633-636.

22. Boscarino, J. A., Adams, R.E. and Figley, C.R. (2005). A prospective cohort study of the effectiveness of employer sponsored crisis intervention after a major disaster, 7 (1), 31-44.

23. Reese, J.T. (1987). *A history of police psychological services.* Washington, DC: US Department of Justice, Federal Bureau of Investigation.

24. Reese, J.T., Horn, J.M. and Dunning, C. (Eds.). (1991). *Critical incidents in policing,* revised. Washington, DC: US Government Printing Office for the US Department of Justice: Federal Bureau of Investigation.

25. Mitchell, J.T. & Bray, G. (1990). *Emergency Services Stress: Guidelines for preserving the health and careers of emergency service personnel.* Englewood Cliffs, NJ: Prentice Hall.

26. Mitchell, J.T. (2005). *The Quick Series Guide to: Stress Management for Emergency Personnel.* Fort Lauderdale, Fl: Luxart Communications.

27. Flannery, R.B. (1998). *The Assaulted Staff Action Program: Coping with the Psychological Aftermath of Violence.* Ellicott City, MD: Chevron Publishing.

28. Roberts, A.R. and Camasso, M. (1994). Staff turnover at crisis intervention units and programs: A national survey. *Crisis Intervention and Time-Limited Treatment,* 1(1), 1-9.

29. Roberts, A.R. (2000). An Overview of Crisis Theory and Crisis Intervention. In A. Roberts (Ed.) *Crisis Intervention Handbook: Assessment, Treatment, and Research.* New York: Oxford University Press.

30. Mitchell, J.T. (2005). Crisis Management. In Robert H. Coombs (Ed.) *Addiction* Counseling Review: Preparing for Comprehensive, Certification and Licensing *Examinations*. Mahwah, NJ: Lawrence Erlbaum Associates, Inc.

31. Lindy, J. (1985). The trauma membrane and other clinical concepts derived from psychotherapeutic work with survivors of natural disasters. *Psychiatric Annals*, 15, 153-160.

32. Kardiner A. and Spiegel, H. (1947). *War, Stress, and Neurotic Illness*. New York: Hoeber.

33. Parad, H. J. (1971). Crisis Intervention. In R. Morris (Ed.) *Encyclopedia of Social Work*, vol. 1, 196-202.

34. Duffy, J. (1979). The role of CMHCs in airport disasters. *Technical Assistance CenterReport*, 2(1), 1; 7-9.

35. Slaikeu, K.A. (1984). *Crisis intervention: A handbook for practice and research*. Boston, MA: Allyn and Bacon, Inc.

36. Everly, G.S., Jr. and Mitchell, J.T. (1997). *Critical Incident Stress Management: A new era and standard of care in crisis intervention*. Ellicott City, MD: Chevron Publishing Corp.

37. Everly G.S., Jr. and Mitchell, J.T. (1998). *Assisting Individuals in Crisis: A Workbook*. Ellicott City, MD: International Critical Incident Stress Foundation.

38. Mitchell, J.T. and Resnik, H.L.P. (1981). *Emergency Response to Crisis*. Englewood Cliffs, NJ: Robert J. Brady Company, Subsidiary of Prentice Hall.

39. Mitchell, J.T. and Resnik, H.L.P. (1986). *Emergency Response to Crisis*. Ellicott City, MD: Chevron Publishing (reprinted from original).

40. Mitchell, J.T. (2004). Characteristics of Successful Early Intervention Programs. *International Journal of Emergency Mental Health*, 6, 4. 175-184.

Chapter 3

Strategic and Tactical Considerations for Crisis Intervention

Concentrate all your thoughts upon the work at hand.
The sun's rays do not burn until brought to a focus.
~ Alexander Graham Bell *(1847 – 1922 Scientist, inventor)*

INTRODUCTION

Haphazard applications of crisis interventions at best accomplish little, and at worst may be more harmful than helpful. This is not just a question about whether or not something should be done in a crisis. Most reasonable people accept the concept that doing something to help others during periods of extreme distress is important. It is more an issue of choosing the correct support service to fit the circumstances and the needs of the people who want assistance and then timing those interventions to achieve the best possible outcome. It is also important to assure that the support services are delivered by people who are properly trained. Training   reduces the potential that negative outcomes could result from the intervention. That approach constitutes a strategic response.

RANGE of ASSISTANCE

Assistance to humans can cover a wide range of activities and behaviors. The term, *casual assistance* refers to the everyday things that people do to make life a little more livable for others. It includes things such as the common courtesies of holding a door for someone, offering a seat to an elderly person on a bus, giving someone directions when he or she is lost, or helping a child get dressed. There are a countless minor behaviors and activities that render assistance to others in a casual manner.

Informal assistance is a more organized approach to helping others. It generally requires some training to accomplish its tasks. Information specialists who work, for example, for a local Chamber of Commerce, a national park, or a community visitor center provide informal assistance. They can provide information, guidance, and directions in a more official setting. Some crisis intervention elements fall under the category of informal assistance. Crisis Management Briefings, for example, are informal "town meetings" where team leaders present useful information.

Formal assistance implies a more structured relationship between the person needing assistance and the one who is providing it. Social service agencies are a good example of organizations that are involved in formal assistance programs on a daily basis. Trained people in these agencies offer a spectrum of services to their clients, such as offering information and financial assistance or assisting people in finding employment. Some elements of crisis intervention are within the formal assistance category.

As suggested in the previous paragraphs, crisis intervention overlaps into both the informal and the formal types of assistance. Crisis intervention is applied when a person's coping resources are challenged or impaired. It is a set of temporary, active, and supportive interventions to stabilize a distressed person or even a group. When peer support personnel provide information and one-on-one support, crisis intervention services are more informal. When mental health professionals work with disaster victims and write up documentation for follow-up, they are functioning within the more formal ranges of crisis intervention. In any case, once stabilization is achieved, the task of the person or crisis team providing the assistance is to mitigate the impact of the disturbing event and to restore people to the highest level of adaptive functioning that is possible under the circumstances.

Institutional care is the most complex of all the types of assistance. It is utilized when a person is no longer capable of caring for themselves or when their needs greatly exceed the capacities of virtually all of the informal and formal methods of providing assistance. This type of care is far beyond the realm of crisis intervention and is provided only by professionals. It is possible for a person's condition to deteriorate so severely that they might need institutional care. That, however, would be a rather rare occurrence.

Obviously, the greater the needs of an individual or a group and the less capable they are of managing themselves, the more complex the formal assistance may become. If a person's needs exceed the resources and capacities of a crisis intervention team, the next higher level of care may be required to provide the appropriate assistance. As a person requires more assistance, they may be moved from the supportive crisis intervention services at one end of the range of assistance to formal therapy or perhaps institutional care at the other end. Table 3.1 offers a diagram of the range of assistance from casual assistance to formal psychotherapy and institutional care. The diagram should **not** be interpreted to mean that every person will progress from informal to formal assistance and eventually to therapy. That is very far from the truth. *The vast majority of people who receive crisis intervention services after exposure to a traumatic event do not need psychotherapy.* The diagram simply shows where crisis intervention fits, within the wide range of available human assistance. Note clearly that crisis intervention is not psychotherapy.

Please note also that there are no clear demarcations between casual assistance and informal assistance, and between informal assistance and formal assistance, and so on. There is some natural overlap between the types of help. Common courtesy should continue even when people need to receive services from other points on the continuum of care. Informal services sometimes overlap with formal services and vice versa.[1-5]

Table 3.1
Range of Assistance

Casual Assistance	Informal Assistance	Formal Assistance	Institutional Care
Assistance in every-day life. Courtesy	Information; Employment; Social Services	Psychological First Aid or Crisis Intervention	Outpatient counseling or Psychotherapy	Inpatient hospitalization; Medication; Medical or psychiatric treatment

TRAUMA RESPONSE and the STAGES of RECOVERY: A Brief Overview

Support services and interventions of any type do not make sense unless one first understands the human reaction to a traumatic event (critical incident). If there is no understanding of what is happening to a person in a state of crisis, the choice of interventions will not match the person's needs. That is the point at which there is a chance of being more harmful than helpful. There are six main stages of response to a highly distressing event.

- Alarm reaction
- Shock and disruption
- The emotional impact
- Coping and repair
- Adaptation
- Learning to live with leftovers

The following paragraphs offer some insight into what is going on in the six main stages of the response to a highly distressing event.

The Alarm Reaction

Once a critical incident occurs the first reaction of the human system is **physical and mental mobilization**. A bath of stress chemicals charges through the body and alerts all physical systems to a heightened state of arousal. The brain responds by increasing the speed of its processing of both stored and new information. Besides enhanced information processing, the brain accelerates its decision-making processes. Decision-making shortcuts not usually available to the brain when unstressed suddenly seem to open up in a brain reacting to a traumatic event. When stressed, the brain seems to react more intuitively, rather than employing its usual cognitive processes

Mild to moderate perceptual distortions are adaptive and quite common and normal during the period of mental mobilization. The following list of perceptual distortions is presented in a descending order from the most common to the least common distortion.

- Time distortion
- Visual distortion
- Auditory distortion
- Slow motion action
- Tunnel vision
- Diminished hearing
- Intensified sound
- Fast motion
- Remembering extreme details

If these distortions become extreme, however, there is a greater chance that the person could develop a mental disorder called Posttraumatic Stress Disorder (PTSD). The literature regarding PTSD suggests that it is the worst of the numerous stress reactions that can result from an exposure to an acute traumatic event. If a person is concerned about perceptual distortions that occurred during a traumatic event, the intensity and duration of perceptual distortions should be discussed with a mental health professional. If things return to normal and a person is not left with significant disturbance after exposure to a traumatic event, there is probably little need to worry.[6, 7, 8]

IMPORTANT STRATEGIC NOTE!

The alarm reaction, with its physical and mental mobilization is all about survival in the face of a threatening or overwhelming event. This is the absolute worst time to attempt to apply crisis interventions of any type. The best we can do is to help the person get the situation resolved. If we cannot do that, then it is best to avoid getting in the way. During the alarm stage the most important focus is doing what one has to do for survival, safety, and resolution of the situation.

Shock and Disruption

When the situation ends, a person may be initially dazed and confused for a period lasting from minutes to several days. Then, there is a rebound effect. This period is sometimes accompanied by physical reactions such as lightheadedness, rapid deep breathing, shakes or tremors, nausea, crying, racing heartbeat, sweating, and chills. The physical reactions are typically **normal responses** to the high level of stress chemicals that naturally pour into the body system during the alarm stage. One should be cautious, however, not to interpret dangerous physical symptoms as "normal." If a person experiences difficulty breathing, chest pain, unusual headaches, or blood in urine or fecal matter, those signs and symptoms require further medical evaluation as quickly as possible.

There are also cognitive and emotional reactions to a traumatic experience. They include denial, disbelief, dissociation, feeling mad, sad, scared, anxious, or sometimes elated. People may also find that they have a hard time shutting off the "auto pilot" and cannot relax. Their memory functions seem to be on "overdrive" or "under-drive;" that is, they remember excessive details of some aspects of the situation and very little or nothing of other aspects of the situation. Some people cannot understand what happened and what significance it has. They also find themselves feeling more agitated, irritable, and over-reactive to minor stimuli. As a result, they may isolate themselves from other people to limit their agitation. Some cannot shut off their memories of the event and have dreams and nightmares about it. Sleep disturbances may result from this hyper-aroused state.

There are many other stress signals that are not listed here. But listing each one would take a considerable amount of space in this book and would not likely contribute much to the objectives of this current discussion. Any signs or symptoms of distress that are severe, prolonged beyond a few weeks, or extremely unusual require further evaluation. They are indicative of more dangerous physical or emotional conditions.[9]

IMPORTANT STRATEGIC NOTES!

- The symptoms and signals of distress in the preceding paragraphs are stress reactions; they are *not signs of weakness*.
- Any signs, symptoms, or signals of distress that become intense or prolonged should be evaluated by a mental health professional.
- Any physical symptoms, such as chest pain, shortness of breath beyond a few minutes, difficulty breathing, or severe headaches, should be evaluated immediately by medical personnel.
- The greatest needs of crisis intervention support in this stage are information, individual support, and a reduction in the level of distress.
- The Critical Incident Stress Debriefing would be *too early in this stage*. It takes 18 to 24 hours for the stress symptoms to decrease sufficiently to allow the cognitive interactions required in a CISD.[10]

The Emotional Impact

The real emotional impact to a traumatic event usually begins a day or two after the event. It most cases it may continue for several days; but for some people it will last weeks or longer. Several factors that influence the duration of the emotional impact are: the situation itself, the coping skills available to the distressed person, and the availability of support services. As pointed out earlier, signs and symptoms of distress whose intensity or duration is unusual should be further evaluated by competent medical or psychological professionals.[11]

IMPORTANT STRATEGIC NOTE!
The emotional impact stage is a crucial stage for the provision of crisis intervention services. What is done to support people in this stage will have far-reaching effects on their recovery over the course of time. If a group is involved, *this is the best stage at which to employ the Critical Incident Stress Debriefing (CISD)*. Individual peer support is the best tactic if an individual is involved. Remember, however, that the CISD is not a stand-alone intervention. Use CISD within the context of a comprehensive, integrated, systematic, and multi-component crisis intervention program applied in a strategic manner.[12]

Coping and repair

In the coping and repair stage of trauma response, the person tries to understand what happened - to work through it and to "come to grips" with the emotional impact of the incident. The cognitive, physical, and emotional reactions generally become more manageable during this stage. Since the focus on the traumatic event itself lessens, people take on a renewed interest in their work and begin to make plans for the future. There might also be attempts to reestablish relationships neglected during the turmoil of the traumatic stress reaction.

This stage is also a time for soul searching. A person struggles with many questions. "What if this had happened? What if I had done something else instead? Why did this happen to me? Could I have prevented this? What will I do the next time? Can I still do my job?" There are so many questions and the answers are not always easy to find.[13]

IMPORTANT STRATEGIC NOTE!
The person or team providing crisis support needs to decide, with the person involved in the crisis reaction, whether or not he or she is ready to face the incident and deal with it or to continue to withdraw for a while more. Crisis intervention tactics

should focus of good listening, information, and an
atmosphere of overall acceptance and support.

Adaptation

In this stage, the person works to accept the reality of the situation and
the feelings of vulnerability that were present during it. There eventually
comes a realization that *vulnerable* does not mean *helpless* and that the person
can control their reactions. Hopefully, the person exposed to the critical incident
will accept that they did the best that could be done under the circumstances.
Recovery is well on the way when the person can recognize that the fear they
experienced is a normal and not a shameful reaction. Finally, the darkness of
the traumatic response lifts when the person accepts the possibility that they
can actually emerge stronger from this situation. Adaptation also involves a
re-evaluation of values, goals, and priorities. The positive side to being exposed
to a terrifying event is that a person can learn valuable lessons that might help
them or others in some future experience.[11, 13]

IMPORTANT STRATEGIC NOTE!

As a person gains greater insight into what has
occurred and how the event has impacted his or her
life, the need for crisis intervention decreases. Crisis
team members should recognize this fact and prepare
to disengage from the person as they improve.
Attempting to hold onto a person as they emerge
from the crisis state and return to as normal a level
of function as possible is self-serving and
counterproductive.

Learning to live with leftovers

Traumatic events leave a mark on a person. The experience of a critical
incident changes a person. It is impossible to return to exactly what life was
like before the critical incident occurred. The only option is to learn to live
with the memories and the aftereffects. New, but similar, experiences can
remind us of a past critical incident and stir some internal discomfort. Situations
that impact others can stimulate emotions in us, even if we are not involved in
the situation ourselves. Anniversary reactions are quite common as well. Those
things will happen and the traumatized person must live with that as a reality
of life. The important thing is not to allow those remembered events to gain
the upper hand and cause us to have uncontrollable emotional reactions.[13]

IMPORTANT STRATEGIC NOTE!

From a crisis intervention point of view, for someone who has reached stage six in the trauma response, the greatest needs are for reassurance and information. Little else is required. If a person appears "stuck" and is unable to complete the six stages of trauma response process, a referral to a professional for further evaluation and possible treatment is the best course of action.

The CRISIS RESPONSE STRATEGY

The "important strategic notes" throughout this chapter touch on various key elements of a crisis strategy. The crisis intervener provides the right type and amount of support at the most crucial times and gradually decreases involvement as the person improves. The following section will further elaborate on the strategy behind crisis intervention tactics.

Strategy involves arranging the available resources and tactics and then timing their implementation to assure the most advantageous circumstances possible. The ultimate goal of a crisis intervention strategy is the successful alleviation of human distress and a restoration of the personnel to the highest level of adaptive function possible given the circumstances.[12]

The Strategic Formula

There is a useful and easy to remember formula to assist crisis interveners in developing the strategic crisis response plan. It is "the five 'T' planning formula;" each of its elements has a label that begins with the letter 'T'. The five 'Ts' are:

- Target
- Type
- Timing
- Theme
- Team

Target refers to the object(s) of the assistance. That is, who needs help? Is it an individual or a group? If it is an individual, what was that person's level of exposure to the traumatic event? What was that person's role in the experience? If the target is a group, is it one group or are there several groups? Is the group a homogeneous group or a heterogeneous group? What is the nature of the group and the relationship of the group members to each other?

Type indicates the "package" of interventions that should be selected from the many tactics in the Critical Incident Stress Management field. Carefully match specific tactics to the requirements of those in need of assistance.

Timing refers to the best time to provide the various types of support services. If the timing is not carefully thought out, it is likely that the interventions will be less effective.

Theme includes the circumstances of the actual event as well as any issue, concern, circumstance, or consideration that might alter decision-making, timing, crisis team makeup, and the types of interventions chosen.

Team identifies the crisis team or resources that will be required to provide the right assistance at the appropriate time. Team relates to size of the team, the gender, age, and background of the team members, and specialty functions required of the team.

Some people add a sixth 'T' to the formula: it is "***Think***." Review and revise plans often. Circumstances change; new information becomes available; additional challenges arise. Crisis interveners must be alert and adjust their intervention "packages" when conditions warrant such changes.[12]

Key Elements of a Strategic Crisis Response

The crisis response strategy should be broad. It should have four key elements. The first is that a crisis response strategy should be **comprehensive**. That is, there should be several elements in place before a crisis strikes to assure that crisis response teams are ready to respond to crisis reactions in others. The second element of a crisis strategy is that it is **integrated**. All the tactics for carrying out the strategy should be linked to one another in a seamless pattern so that one does not interfere with another. The third element of a strategic crisis response plan is that the program of crisis intervention must be **systematic**. There are logical steps when applying a crisis response strategy. The first step is assessment of the situation and the reactions of the people involved. The next logical step is to develop a response plan based on "the five 'T's" described above. Then apply the crisis intervention tactics according to priorities and in the right timeframe. In many situations, individual support precedes small group support services. A defusing can be provided on the same day as the traumatic experience and then followed, several days later, by a Critical Incident Stress Debriefing. These are just a few examples of strategic decision making in response to crisis. The last of the four elements of strategic response is that it must be ***multi-component***. No workman would use the same tool for every job he encountered. Likewise, in the field of crisis intervention, there are many different crisis tools. Each tool is selected for its specific purposes.[14]

Table 3.2

Strategic Crisis Response

Time Frame	Activities
First hours	Assess
	Develop a strategy
	Psychological First Aid
	• Safety / protection
	• Food, water, shelter
	• Reduce arousal
	• Mobilize resources
	• Facilitate primary groups
	• Provide information
	• Encourage communications
	• Communicate to people about risks of exposure or injury and suggest how people might limit their risks
	• Active listening
	• Nutrition, sleep, rest
	• Refer if necessary
	• Follow-up if indicated
	Target
	Types
	Timing
	Themes
	Team

First 24 hours

Think!

Tactics must match people's needs

Tactics need to be appropriate to
circumstances

Demobilization (if emergency personnel
are involved in a disaster)

Crisis Management Briefing

Defusing (small homogeneous group)

5 phase CISD (for suicide of a colleague
or Line of duty death)

Individual support

Advice and counsel to supervisors and
administrators

24 hours to 5 days

Think!

Review and revise the strategic plan

Individual support

Family support

Critical Incident Stress Debriefing

Follow-up services

Continue Psychological First Aid

Continue advice and counsel to
supervisors and administrators

Information and guidance

5 to 14 days

Think!

Review and revise the strategic plan

Assess to determine additional needs

Assess to determine effectiveness of
previous interventions

Individual interventions

Referrals if determined necessary

Eye Movement Desensitization and Reprocessing (EMDR)

Cognitive Behavioral Therapy (CBT)

Identification of additional resources

Information / Education

Lessons learned

2 weeks to 52 weeks   Think!

Review and revise the strategic plan

Assess effectiveness of services to date / additional needs

Follow up on referrals

Follow up meetings

Disengage if recovery is complete

Individual support if necessary

Draw lesson form the experience

Post Critical Incident Stress Seminars

Assist at time of anniversaries as necessary

"Give Some, Get Some!"

Some military combat stress specialists use the phrase, "Give some, get some!" to encourage their personnel to give help to others, but remember to take care of themselves as well. Without doubt, many crisis intervention tactics can help others. It would be a serious mistake, however, to have a strategic crisis response plan that does not include numerous stress management tactics for self-care as well. Both tactics to help others and tactics to help oneself or the members of one's crisis team will be detailed in the sections to follow.[15]

CRISIS and STRESS MANAGEMENT TACTICS for OTHERS

General Crisis Tactics for Others:

- Identify potential at risk populations.
- Identify and establish linkages with community resources
- Educate the public.

- Develop comprehensive, integrated, systematic, and multi-component crisis management programs for the community.

- Develop an understanding of ethnic and cultural reactions to crisis that might influence the choice and application of crisis tactics.

- Develop community response plans before crises strike.

- When a traumatic event occurs, gather information regarding the impacted population and meet with community leaders before deciding on a plan of action.

- Develop and maintain open lines of communication with leaders in the community.

- Suggest site management procedures to limit stressors in the environment.

- Use the *five "T" planning formula* to develop a comprehensive, integrated, systematic, and multi-component program for rendering assistance.[16, 17, 18]

Specific Crisis Tactics for Others:
Caring for the victims of tragedy

- Protect the victims from further stress, such as the media, curiosity seekers, gory sights and sounds, or additional unnecessary exposures to the horror of the incident.

- Mobilize the resources necessary to assist the victims, such as the Red Cross or other disaster services.

- Help the victims to find missing family members and friends.

- Regroup families.

- Regroup people who come from the same areas.

- Listen carefully to the victims. They need opportunities to express themselves.

- Accurate, current, and timely information is extremely important to the well being of victims. **Information is by far one of the most crucial forms of psychological first aid.**

- Reassure people that they are safe.

- Establish private quarters for the victims as soon a possible.

- Provide for medical, social, religious, psychological, and other needs as they arise.

- Provide food, water, warmth, shelter, and opportunities for rest and sleep.
- Do not tell victims that they are "lucky, because it could have been worse." Those sorts of statements almost never console and usually anger a distressed person.
- Gently touch a distressed person on the shoulder or hand if they seem receptive to such contact.
- Keep yourself calm and your voice soothing and reassuring.
- Evacuate a shocked, very silent, and withdrawn person from the scene immediately. They tend to be in the first priority group for evacuation and intervention.
- Although we tend to pay attention to noisy, hysterical, or acting out victims, they are actually a secondary priority. It is better for them to express themselves than to be extremely silent and withdrawn, although they may tend to interfere with the operations.
- Those who seem to be doing fine at the scene are the third priority for evacuation. Being a third priority, however, does not imply that they should be ignored. They can get worse if they are unattended.
- Children are the most vulnerable to psychological harm during a disaster. Afford special care to children. [8, 18, 19,]

Stress Control Measures for First Responders: Tactics That Can Help *Before* the Critical Incident

- Obtain education and information on critical incidents, critical incident stress, and the crisis response. Informed people are better able to manage critical incident stress when it strikes.
- Make certain that policies and procedures for CISM are in place.
- Establish a well-trained CISM team and make sure that it is trained to provide a variety of services to individuals and groups under different circumstances.

Stress Control Measures for First Responders: Tactics That Can Help *During* the Critical Incident

- Calm yourself before deployment. Try some deep breaths to provide yourself with a few seconds to think how you are going to approach the situation.

- The action taken while involved in a situation can help to focus stress reactions into usable energy; but try not to become overwhelmed by the intense stimuli of the situation.

- Take frequent breaks. Brief rest periods, some food, and fluids can help to keep you alert during a mission.

- Actual work periods may vary from situation to situation. There are some general rules that can be helpful for supervisors. Typically, a two hour work period is followed by a half hour of down time. Intense cold or heat or the intensity of the scene itself may cause alterations in the deployment cycles.

- One half day off after every five days and a full day off after ten consecutive days of disaster work can help to keep people functional.

- Remind yourself that you have the skills to carry out the mission.

- A sense of humor helps. Be careful, however, not to use humor too much or when it is inappropriate, such as in the presence of the actual victims of the event. They will not understand or appreciate your humor.

- Do not over-control your emotions. A brief and controlled discharge of emotions is healthier than completely suppressing your emotions, which may hurt you later.

- It is suggested that the use of caffeinated products be limited during prolonged and intense work, such as disaster work. If total elimination is not possible, a considerable reduction in the use of caffeinated products should then be the aim.

- Alcohol should be avoided altogether since it interferes with Rapid Eye Movement (REM) sleep patterns. REM sleep helps us to mentally process the traumatic events of the last few days. When alcohol interferes with REM sleep, one of nature's best ways of managing life's tragedies is eliminated and the person is then more vulnerable to the negative aftereffects of a traumatic exposure.

- Eat when you can, even if you don't feel like it. You need energy.

- Avoid too much sugar, foods high in fat content, processed foods, and white bread. They add little to nutrition and most often complicate the stress reaction.

- Eat balanced meals with some proteins, complex carbohydrates, and some fruits and vegetables.

- In a prolonged incident, 8-hour shifts are preferable. If unusual circumstances require longer time commitments, the maximum is 12 hours of work. The alternation of 12 hours on duty, then 12 hours off duty is a good formula to maintain a healthy work force.

- It is helpful to remind people of the time as they work at any prolonged situation. The reminders help people to stay oriented and focused.

- No one should get less than four hours of sleep in 24 hours. "Four in twenty four" cannot, however, become the persistent rule. It is an exception to the rule and it is applied only in unusual circumstances. If it goes on for too many days, health problems can arise. Obviously, 7 to 8 hours of sleep per night is the ideal.

- Limit exposures to gory sights and disturbing sounds and smells.

- Disengage non-essential personnel from the scene as soon as possible.

- Rotate personnel to various duties whenever possible so that they do not feel that they are stuck on one assignment indefinitely.

- It is best to rotate people from high stress operations to moderately stressful work before moving them to rest areas. People also adjust better to intense work situations when they have been moved from rest to moderately stressful work and then onto highly stressful work.

- Handling human remains and personal effects is extremely stressful work; the people doing that work need frequent breaks and emotional support. Rotate personnel off these duties to other assignments whenever possible.

- Call in supportive resources such as Critical Incident Stress Management teams and chaplains to assist one's personnel according to the needs expressed by the operations personnel.

- On scene support services must be carefully trained to maintain a low key and unobtrusive presence. They should never interfere with ongoing operations. Support services in the field should focus on providing advice to supervisors and assisting individuals who appear to be having significant reactions to the emergency services work. In some situations direct crisis intervention services are provided to the primary victims and survivors of the incident until other resources can be obtained to assist those people. [8]

Stress Control Measures for First Responders: Tactics That Can Help *After* the Critical Incident

- Rest
- Eat nutritious meals

- Physical exertion exercise helps to reduce the chemicals of distress in a person's body. Even walking can be very helpful. However, no one should do physical exercise if they are not physically able to do so.

- Attend group support services when they are offered by a trained CISM team. They can "take the edge off" of a bad incident. But, most importantly, they can be extremely helpful for other members of one's group. Everyone gets a sense of the "big picture" and comments made by one member of the group often clarify the experience for other members of the group.

- Restore normal routines as soon as possible.

- Keep yourself active. Do not permit boredom to set in.

- Express your feelings to people you trust.

- Dreams and memories of the tragedy are common. They generally decrease over several weeks time. If they remain intense after three weeks to a month has passed, seek out CISM team members for assistance and/or a referral for professional care.

- Do not joke with fellow workers about the tragedy too much. Some people are sensitive to the experience and may have not fully recovered.

- Do not engage in unproductive criticism of others. If mistakes were made during the incident and corrective action or additional training is required, that can be handled by the organization's leadership; but individual members of the organization do not help their fellow workers by constantly bringing up mistakes made by colleagues.

- Anger is a frequent emotion after the intensity of a major event. Do not take it personally. It should subside in a reasonable time. If not, the angry person may need some additional assistance to get things back under control.

- Focus on the here and now. Telling old war stories of events that were worse than the current event is not always helpful to the people who only have the recent experience to relate to.

- Listen to those who want to talk about their experience.

- Shedding tears after a painful event is perfectly normal; but frequent uncontrolled crying spells accompanied by sleep disturbance and an inability to return to normal duties is an indication that a person needs assistance from a CISM team or a mental health professional.

- Help each other. Try to understand and care for each other. No one can support you as well as one who does the same work. If people are careless with the feelings of others then the opposite rule applies. That is, no one can hurt you more than someone who does the same type of work.[20, 21, 22]

Care for the Caretakers:
The Post Action Staff Support Program

Once a critical incident stress team has completed its assignment of supporting others, it must turn its attention to caring for itself. Without some self-care a critical incident stress team will feel depleted and lack energy. It will be unable to learn useful lessons from its experience and it will be ill- prepared to engage in future support services. Team self-care falls under the label, Post Action Staff Support (PASS). There are many possible aspects of a PASS program, as the following lists suggests. It is not an exhaustive list by any means. Accomplishing every item on the list is not important. Some things will make sense under certain circumstances, but not under others. What is important is that there is a practical plan to support crisis team members after they have supported others. Some events will require very little beyond a brief conversation between a team coordinator or clinical director and the response team itself. The more complex and prolonged the incident, the greater will be the need for a structured Post Action Staff Support program as is suggested below.

1. Greet team members who are returning from a mission, especially if the mission was prolonged. Team members can be met at the airport or at a designated meeting spot.

2. Information and guidelines should be provided to CISM team member families during the deployment and as well as afterwards.

3. Individual support should be arranged for team members who were more seriously impacted by their support work in the traumatic event.

4. A modified group CISD can be designed for team members after serving in a support role in a traumatic event. Here is one possible approach:

   - Present a brief introduction, welcoming the team members back from the deployment.

   - Let people know that the CISD they will go through will be a loose adaptation of the standard CISD process.

   - Remind people that the usual rules of confidentiality must be observed.

- Ask the team members to state their names and their functions while deployed.

- Keep it casual and conversational. Back and forth comments, explanations, or clarifications, and even quips or other types of appropriate humor may be helpful. Do not try to be humorous if there is nothing funny about what they are saying. Add clarifying questions if you think they will help to move the conversation along.

- Ask about any key thoughts they had when they were first asked to go on the deployment and how those thoughts may have changed as they proceeded through the experience. Round out that section by asking if they have any prominent thoughts now that the deployment has concluded. Acknowledge and respond to some of the thoughts as you would when engaged in conversations with friends.

- Ask if there is anything about the deployment that will stick with them for some time to come. Another way to bring issues into the conversation is to ask if anything about the experience touched their own heart strings as they did their work in the field.

- Make inquiries about how well they think they performed as individuals and as team members.

- Ask how people reacted to their work and whether they feel people benefited from what they did.

- If they did CISDs, ask how those interventions went.

- Ask about complications or unusual circumstances that the crisis team members had to work under during the deployment.

- Ask if they returned from the deployment with any stress-related symptoms or signals of personal distress.

- Ask what they would like to do differently in the future.

- Inquire about how well or poorly the team that remained at home supported their efforts in the field and if any changes need to be made in team protocols or procedures.

- Ask what key points they have learned and how the experience might help them in future CISM work.

- Ask how the team members might have grown from the experience and what, if any, positive influences the deployment might have on them in the future.

- Ask if there were any unusual, humorous, or even bizarre circumstances that occurred while they were deployed.

- If you are truly having a collegial discussion, you will have been teaching all through the discussion. Therefore, in the teaching phase, you should spend time going over any important recovery and resiliency issues that may not have been fully covered in the main body of the CISD.

- Finally, wrap up the session. Be sure to thank everyone for the work they did and for their participation in the session. Thanking, acknowledging, appreciating, and encouraging your colleagues is what this session is all about.

- Anyone who appears to need more than the session could provide should be seen individually. If necessary, referrals can be made to help people complete any unfinished business.

5. Provide a case review meeting in which the activities of the crisis team members are reviewed with the goal of learning important lessons so that the team can improve future interventions.

6. Make sure individual follow-ups are available to determine that the team members are recovering and able to return to normal work and family duties and responsibilities.

7. Educational sessions should be provided for other teams to promote a wide distribution of information that can be helpful in preparing people to respond to future tragedies.

8. For some, memorial services or religious ceremonies may be helpful in putting the tragic event in perspective.

9. Meetings with organizational, municipal, state, or federal officials can be held to review and acknowledge the work of the team members and to make plans for future situations.

10. Dinners, cook-outs, social events, thank you notes, certificates, flowers, and awards to those who served others so graciously will go far to enhance team spirit and maintain maximum team performance.

When the PASS program is finished people on the crisis response team should feel valued and appreciated for their talents and their efforts. The PASS program should help them to return to normal life functions.[23]

SUMMARY

This chapter presented an overview of the categories of assistance and important trauma and recovery phases, before detailing a strategic crisis response plan. The steps in developing a crisis-oriented strategy were covered. They are Target, Type, Timing, Theme, and Team.

The strategic crisis response plan was described as having four key elements. The strategy should be comprehensive, integrated, systematic and multi-component. Extensive portions of the chapter provided detailed lists of crisis intervention tactics that are useful for the general public as well as specific lists for emergency responders.

Finally, the chapter noted the importance of taking care of the crisis team that managed the traumatic stress response for others. Specific guidelines for taking care of team members were provided.

In the next chapter, *The Value of Groups*, we look at the foundations of group interventions. We will review their history, effects, and current status. That chapter will lay the final foundation for subsequent chapters describing specific group support services and providing detailed instructions on how to apply the most important group crisis intervention tactics.

REFERENCES - Chapter 3

1. Caplan, G. Killilea, M. (Eds.) (1976) *Support Systems and Mutual Help: Multidisciplinary Explorations.* New York: Grune and Stratton.

2. Cook, J.A., Heller, T., & Pickett-Schenk, S.A. (1999). The effects of Support Group Participation on Caregiver Burden Among Parents of Adult Offspring with Severe Mental Illness. *Family Relations, 48,* 405-410.

3. Salby, A.E., Lieb, J., & Tancredi, L.R. (1975). *Handbook of Psychiatric Emergencies.* New York: Medical Examination Publishing Company, Inc.

4. Samuels, M. & Samuels, D. (1975). *The complete Handbook of Peer Counseling:* An authoritative guide for the organization, training,

implementation and evaluation of a peer counseling program. Miami FL: Fiesta Publishing Corporation.

5. Swanson, W.C., & Carbon, J.B. (1989). Crisis intervention: Theory and Technique. In Task Force Report of the American Psychiatric Association. *Treatments of Psychiatric Disorders.* Wash. D.C.: APAPress.

6. Selye, H. (1956). *The Stress of Life.* New York: Free Press.

7. Wilson J. and Keane, T. (1997). *Assessing Psychological Trauma and PTSD.* New York: Guilford Press.

8. Mitchell, J.T. & Bray, G. (1990). *Emergency Services Stress: Guidelines for preservingthe health and careers of emergency service personnel.* Englewood Cliffs, NJ: Prentice Hall.

9. Holding, D.H. Fatigue. (1983). In G.R.J. Hockey (Ed). Stress and Fatigue in Human Performance. New York: John Wiley and Sons, Ltd.

10. Gilmartin, K.M. (2002). *Emotional survival for Law Enforcement: A guide for Officers and their families.* Tucson, AZ: E-S Press.

11. Solomon, R. (1991). The dynamics of Fear in Critical Incidents: Implications for Training and Treatment. In James T. Reese, James M. H o r n and Christine Dunning (Eds.) *Critical Incidents in Policing, Revised.* Washington, DC: U.S. Department of Justice, Federal   Bureau of Investigation.

12. Mitchell, J.T. Everly, G.S. & Clark, D. W. (2006). *Strategic Response to Crisis: Student Manual.* Ellicott City, MD: International Critical Incident Stress Foundation.

13. Solomon, Roger, Developer of the Post Critical Incident Seminars for Law Enforcement (August 20, 2006). Personal communication.14. Everly, G.S., Jr. & Mitchell, J.T. (1999). *Critical Incident Stress*Management: A new era and standard of care in crisis intervention. Ellicott City, MD: Chevron Publishing Corp.

15. Wood, Charles, Lt. Colonel, United States Air Force, Air National Guard, (2004). Personal Communication.

16. Slaikeu, K.A. (1984). *Crisis intervention: A handbook for practice and research.* Boston, MA: Allyn and Bacon, Inc..

17. Farberow, N.L., & Frederick, C.J. (1978).Disaster relief workers burnout syndrome. Field Manual for Human Service Workers in Major Disasters. Washington, DC: US Government Printing Office.

18. Neil, T., Oney, J., DiFonso, L., Thacker, B., & Reichart, W. (1974). *Emotional First Aid.* Louisville: Kemper-Behavioral Science Associates.

19. Everly, G.S., Jr. (1999). Emergency Mental Health: An Overview. *International Journal of Emergency Mental Health*, 1, 3-7.

20. Mitchell, J.T. (2005). *The Quick Series Guide to Stress Management for Military personnel.* Fort Lauderdale, Fl: Luxart Communications.

21. Mitchell, J.T. (2005). *The Quick Series Guide to Stress Management for Emergency Personnel.* Fort. Lauderdale, FL: Luxart Communications.

22. Mitchell, J.T. (2002). Stress Management. Course handout material. *Integrated Emergency management Course.* Emergency Management Institute, Federal Emergency Management Agency, Department of Homeland Security.

23. Potter, D. & LaBerteaux, P. (2001) Debriefing the Debriefers. In G.S. Everly and J.T. Mitchell, *Critical Incident Stress Management: Advanced Group Crisis Interventions, a Workbook, Second Edition.* Ellicott City, MD: International Critical Incident Stress Foundation.

Chapter 4

The Value of Groups

"No man is an island, entire of itself;
every man is a piece of the continent."
~ John Donne *(Poet, 1572-1631) Devotions, 1624*

INTRODUCTION

Human beings are social by nature. They have always been so throughout history. They develop families together, hunt in groups, grow crops as a group, and live in communities. Together they build ships, planes, roads, bridges, and buildings. Human beings work together for mutual defense and they fight together as armies. They often share resources and possessions to achieve together what they would be unable to accomplish alone. There are recognized exceptions, such as hermits and mystics who prefer an independent life, essentially devoid of contact with other human beings. But, for the vast majority of human beings, group contact is important, valued, and necessary. Belonging to and being accepted by one or more groups is essential for physical health and psychological well being.

The fact that humans are group-oriented does not mean that groups are always easy to deal with or easy to assist in times of crisis. In fact, groups are complex interrelationships between people. Understanding what groups are and how they function together can enhance crisis intervention services with them and it can assure a greater potential that the group members will recover from a traumatic experience and remain functional and healthy in their personal and work lives.

This chapter is not, by any means, an exhaustive work on groups. Other authors have already written those books. This chapter aims at describing groups in relatively simple terms and providing a working understanding of the history and effectiveness of structured and supportive group interventions.

NATURE of GROUPS

"A group is defined as two or more individuals… who are united by a common interest, characteristic or attachment and whose actions are interrelated." [1] When we define a group, we typically think of a number of people who relate to each other as if they were "together," "united," or as if they were "one." People functioning together as a group demand a certain amount of attention from others. [2]

TYPES of GROUPS

To strategically plan the right interventions for people in a crisis state, we must know if we are dealing with individuals or with groups. Furthermore, if we are assisting a group, we need to know if the group is a primary group, a secondary group, or a random gathering of people.

Primary Groups

There are two *main* types of groups. The first type is a primary group. **Primary groups are groups in which the members have warm, personal ties with one another.** Primary groups are usually small, homogeneous, and their members are dedicated to fairly specific common goals. Contacts are frequent and normally accepting and supportive of the group members. Families, friends, gangs, teams, clubs, classes, church committees, and close-knit work groups, such as emergency and military units are primary groups. Some people might be surprised by the mention of gangs in the list of primary groups. Even self-centered and cruel-minded people will seek out other like-minded people to help them achieve their own goals. They, therefore, form primary groups that have many of the characteristics of other primary groups. Primary groups have these characteristics:

- Several individuals are united as a unit.
- They are thought of as a unit or as if one.
- Members are in relatively frequent contact with one another.
- Members take one another into account and mutually support each other. *The relationship between group members is the one feature that singles out primary groups from secondary groups.*
- The members have significant commonality in interests, beliefs, tasks, training, procedures, and regulations that guide their activities.

- Members believe that the common bonds between them make their group stand out as different from other groups of people.[3]

Secondary Group

Secondary groups are larger, less specific groups in which the members are more "cool" or impersonal toward each other. Contacts between group members are more intermittent and often on a contractual or formal basis. There is a far greater degree of heterogeneity in secondary groups. *They do not have the relationship links that are so characteristic of primary groups.* They are more loosely bonded and their goals are more general. Professional associations, armies, school systems, and large corporations are examples of secondary groups. Some primary groups are part of a secondary group. For example, a well-organized platoon is a primary group but it is part of an army which is a secondary group [3]

Random Groups

Random "groups" are not really groups in the true sense of the word. *Instead, they are gatherings of people who have very little that bond them together.* They are only thought of as a "group" because they share some space during some certain period of time. Either they do not know each other or they have barely an acquaintance relationship with each other. Their contacts are sporadic and impersonal. They do not support each others' efforts on a personal basis and they do not share a common goal. *There is no real relationship between the group members.* In fact, the term *group* is only very loosely applied to them and is generally taken to mean an aggregate, a general category, or a collective. Travelers on a plane or train, shoppers in a mall, the audience in a theatre, or a crowd on a street are all random groups.[3]

BENEFITS of GROUP INTERVENTION

The question, "Why group support instead of all individual assistance?" triggers a number of responses. There are some who suggest that support services, such as Psychological First Aid, and psychotherapy should only be given to individuals. But that attitude denies the social nature of human beings and increases the chance that some people in a crisis will receive services while others receive none. Here are several good reasons why we should be interested in working with groups to help manage crisis reactions.

- The costs are lower.
- Fewer support personnel are required.

- The number of people needing assistance may far exceed number of available support staff.

- Small groups provide good screening opportunities.

- Social support is accepted as enormously helpful by a majority of people in a state of crisis.

- Group members can help each by education and normalization, and in other ways that cannot be achieved in individual contacts.

- Group interventions have a long history of being effective for a wide spectrum of problems.[4]

HISTORY of GROUP INTERVENTIONS

The literature on structured group interventions extends back more than 100 years. In fact, it parallels the historical roots of the field of crisis intervention that were described in Chapter 2 of this book.[2-7] Pioneers in group interactions included such notables as Max Weber and Emile Durkheim, true giants in the field of sociology, and the originator of the psychoanalytic field, Sigmund Freud.[8, 9, 10]

In the early 1900s, group psychotherapy and group processes rapidly moved out of their sociological and psychoanalytic roots and into numerous branches of mainstream social work and psychological practice. Families and children in need of social services were the most prominent groups through the late 1930s. [11, 12, 13]

Interest in family groups and children continued without interruption during World War II and into the present; but considerable attention has turned toward studying and understanding groups of people exposed to the tremendous pressures of war. It was important to know, during those troubled times, how groups, particularly military groups, interacted and reacted while under combat situations. It was also important to identify leadership characteristics that would, most likely, be followed by group members under duress.[14-18] It was during World War II that group crisis intervention services were successfully introduced under less than ideal conditions. Group crisis intervention supportive services were offered to troops during lulls in combat in World War II. They were helpful in reducing combat stress symptoms, as well as in enhancing unit cohesion and unit performance.[19, 20, 21]

After World War II, the Veterans Administration was struggling to cope with the enormous needs of veterans returning from combat. Various group support services were introduced to help them overcome the stresses of combat. One method was the intensive process groups called "encounter groups."[22]

Another method was S. L. A. Marshall's debriefing of the historical aspects of the combat experience. He reported that the soldiers seemed relieved after telling their stories.[23]

In 1947, Kurt Lewin introduced the idea of training people in human relations within work groups. The encounter group movement grew out of his work. The National Training Laboratories (NTL) was formed to provide intensive group process training to people in business and industry. Group process training emphasizes an understanding of the communication patterns and interactions between group members. When those patterns become clear, leaders within organizations can influence and guide group activities to better achieve group objectives and to enhance group productivity. These commercial entities found the group process leadership training programs very helpful to top leaders within corporations. Various challenging social, business, community, church, and school issues were faced and many solutions evolved during the group training programs. Although encounter groups are no longer conducted, the NTL is still active in providing process training to various types of organizations today.[22, 24]

Another early innovative development in the use of group crisis intervention was group work with distressed families struggling through a crisis situation.[25] Crisis intervention services with families were found to be effective in reducing the number of people who entered a hospital for psychiatric treatment. They also reduced the duration of hospitalization in the cases where hospitalization was necessary.[26, 27]

Crisis intervention methods in the emergency services were most often provided on an individual, "one-on-one" basis through the mid 1970s. Crisis intervention techniques for groups were introduced as a part of Critical Incident Stress Management (CISM) programs in the mid 1970s and 1980s. The utilization of non-psychiatric crisis *support groups* was widely considered an innovative advance in the field of crisis intervention. *Unlike psychotherapy groups, support groups do not attempt to achieve personality changes or alterations in deep-seated psychological problems. Instead, in support groups, participants are urged to resist distress and to focus on their personal resiliency, that is, the ability to "bounce back" after a traumatic event. They are encouraged not only to recover their usual psychological balance but to adapt to the circumstances and challenges they are facing.[3]* CISM programs incorporated both large and small group support procedures as just a few of the many elements in an effective crisis intervention system.[28 - 31]

In the past 100 years, the use of group psychotherapy and group support services has spread rapidly to almost every field of human endeavor and throughout most of the world's countries. Group crisis support personnel are constantly learning new lessons and incorporating innovations into the group crisis intervention field.

The group support experience of the last century teaches us many lessons. One fundamental lesson is that group crisis intervention services must be strategic in their applications. Although group crisis intervention can be very helpful in reducing distress and restoring the cohesiveness and performance levels of a primary group, it must be recognized that group crisis intervention has it limitations. The best of group crisis intervention services are always provided within the context of a comprehensive, integrated, systematic, and multi-component program. Additionally, effective group crisis intervention can best be provided by people who are adequately trained and who know how, why, when, and under what circumstances the group services should be applied.[32 - 36]

FOUNDATIONS of CRISIS SUPPORT GROUPS

Today, crisis support groups have four principal underpinnings. They do not stand in isolation from the foundations that have been established in the following disciplines:

- Community psychology[37]
- Crisis intervention[38]
- Group psychotherapy and group processes [39, 40]
- Peer support [41, 42]

Group crisis support incorporates the theory base, history, principles, practices, and procedures, as well as the extensive body of research in all four fields. The evidence-based research from these four fields strongly supports the principles, guidelines, and procedures and practices of crisis support for groups.

DOES GROUP INTERVENTION WORK?

The overwhelming majority of research studies to date on the issue of group psychotherapy and group intervention indicate positive effects. In two distinct reviews on group effectiveness (one study reviewed 700 studies and the second was a meta-analysis of 150 studies) the conclusions were that group psychotherapy and group interventions consistently produced positive effects even with a wide variety of problems and different types of group models.[43, 44, 45, 46]

Irvin D. Yalom, an internationally renowned expert in group process and group psychotherapy, states that "*Group therapy is a potent modality producing significant benefit to its participants...there is considerable evidence that group therapy is at least as efficacious as individual therapy...group therapy was more effective than individual therapy in 25 percent of the studies.* In the other 75 percent, there were *no significant differences* between group and individual therapy. In no study was individual therapy more effective...clients learn to enhance self-efficacy better from peers than from individual therapy."[47]

The number of positive outcome studies in the field of psychotherapy is indeed impressive. It would be a monumental task to describe them all. Even a comprehensive summary of the studies is not possible in the limited space available in this chapter.[39, 40] The following paragraphs, therefore, summarize just a small portion of the research on group psychotherapy, self-help, and mutual aid groups. Mental health professionals conducted the group psychotherapy programs. The self-help and mutual aid group studies represent groups in which non-professionals essentially ran the group with some guidance from a mental health professional. These studies relate best to group crisis support, which utilizes a peer-run, clinician-guided approach. They are most closely aligned with the small group interventions that are described in later chapters in this book.

The literature on group psychotherapy presents consistently positive results.[48] For example, child sexual assault survivors treated in psychotherapy groups improved substantially more than children treated on an individual basis while waiting for an available space in a group treatment program. Furthermore, the groups in which the members were encouraged to support each other maintained the improvements for a period of over six months.[49]

After Hurricane Iniki in Hawaii, elementary school children were treated in individual sessions or in group therapy sessions. Individuals and group members improved more than untreated children who were awaiting treatment. There were no significant differences between those receiving individual treatment and those receiving group treatment. Children involved in individual therapy, however, dropped out of therapy at higher rates than did children treated in groups.[50]

Female sexual assault victims who were treated in groups improved about equally with victims treated in individual sessions. Either treatment proved to be better than no intervention for those who were awaiting treatment.[51]

Symptoms of Posttraumatic Stress Disorder, depression, and psychosocial dysfunction were reduced in both children who were exposed to violence in the community and in adult females who were sexually assaulted. Improvements in group treatment surpassed those who were untreated while waiting to begin treatment.[52, 53]

Group therapy has been very effective in helping clients manage anxiety.[54] Group intervention has also achieved considerable success in helping group members control their panic attacks.[55]

The literature on self-help, mutual aid, and support groups is also quite positive. In fact, several studies indicate a long-term positive effect. One study pointed to positive outcomes from support groups three years or more later.[56] Participation in self-help or mutual aid groups is associated with enhanced feelings of self-efficacy, positive motivation for personal change, and better coping.[57]

Group support programs were effective in smoking cessation and in keeping recovering alcohol and drug users from relapsing into drug use. Several of these studies were Randomized Controlled Trials, which offer the most vigorous evaluations.[58, 59, 60]

Less severe depression and grief were experienced by elderly people who attended peer-run self-help groups than those bereaved individuals who did not attend. [61] Bereaved women who sought assistance after the death of their husband were randomly assigned to professional psychotherapy or to a peer-run support group. Stress and depression decreased equally in both groups.[62] Self-help groups were superior to individual psychotherapy for parents who experienced the death of a child.[63]

In a rather dramatic study of women with breast cancer, 50 of 86 women were given a support group in addition to their medical care. Those who participated in the support group lived twice as long as those women who received only medical care. The average life extension for those in the support group was 18 months longer than the women receiving only medical treatment.[64]

Even via computer messaging to one another, support groups demonstrated significant positive impact. Information and supportive messages were exchanged by email. The young mothers in a study were compared to themselves before and after the support group. Stress decreased in the presence of the support group as positive feelings of belonging to a social network increased. [65]

The sampling of studies with crisis intervention support groups suggests a number of positive outcomes in various populations. For instance, family crisis intervention services were quite successful in reducing child abuse and neglect. [66] Participants in weight loss self-help groups achieved the same benefits as those in groups run by professionals. The cost for the self-help group was half of the cost for the professionally run group.[67] Even in cases of debilitating mental disorders, people who participated in self-help groups had improved coping skills and fewer psychiatric hospitalizations.[68]

"Thus, the best available evidence indicates that group-based psychotherapy is not simply cost-effective but also effective in the field and efficacious in carefully controlled studies."[69]

Yalom summarizes the benefit of support groups with this remark. "Members of such support groups may benefit psychologically, emotionally, and even physically as a result of the group's support for meaningful engagement with life challenges."[70]

SUMMARY

This chapter helped to define **group** and it provided an overview of the types of groups and the general benefits of group intervention. A brief history of group interventions opened up the discussion of whether group interventions could claim any positive effects.

Only a small sampling of the studies on support groups were presented in this chapter. Additional studies on group interventions, especially those associated specifically with critical incident stress, will be presented in subsequent chapters. Readers desiring further information regarding studies on group psychotherapy and self-help support groups should read Irvin Yalom's book, *The Theory and Practice of Group Psychotherapy, 5th Edition* or Leon Schein et al., *Psychological Effects of Catastrophic Disaster: Group Approaches to Treatment*. These two books represent the two most comprehensive volumes written to date on group intervention.

In the next chapter we will gain insight into the inner workings of groups. If we understand how groups work, we can make our own crisis support groups work better.

REFERENCES - Chapter 4

1. Wolman, B. B. (Ed.) (1973). *Dictionary of Behavioral Science*. New York: Van Nostrand Reinhold Company.

2. Small, A. W. (1905). *General Sociology*. Chicago, IL: University of Chicago Press.

3. Olmstead, M.S. Hare, A. P. (1978). *The Small Group, 2nd edition*. New York: Random House.

4. Burlingame, G.M., Mackenzie, K.R. & Strauss, B. (2003). Small group treatment: Evidence for Effectiveness and mechanisms of change. In M. Lambert, A.E. Bergin & S.L. Garfield (Eds.) *Handbook of Psychotherapy and behavior change*, 5th edition. New York: John Wiley and Sons, 647-696.

5. Cooley, C. H. (1909). *Social Organization.* New York: Charles Scribner.

6. Lewin, K. (1948). *Resolving Social Conflicts: Selected Papers on Group Dynamics.* New York: Harper & Row.

7. Davies, D.R., Burlingame, G.M, & Layne, C.M. (2006). Integrating mall-Group Process Principles into Trauma-Focused Group Psychotherapy: What Should a Group Trauma Therapist Know? In L. A. Schein, H. I. Spitz, G. M. Burlingame and P. R. Muskin (Eds). *Psychological* Effects of Catastrophic Disasters: Group Approaches to Treatment. New York: The Haworth Press, 385-423.

8. Parsons, T. (1947). Max Weber. *The Theory of Social and Economic Organization.* New York: Oxford University Press.

9. Durkheim, E. (1947). *The Division of Labor in Society.* Glencoe, IL: Free Press.

10. Freud, S. (1948). *Group Psychology and the analysis of the Ego.* International Psychoanalytic Library. London: Hogarth Press.

11. Strodtbeck, F. L. (1954). The Family as a Three Person Group. *American Sociological Review,* XIX (February), 23-29.

12. Leik, R. K. (1970). Instrumentality and Emotionality in Family Interaction. In T. M. Mills & S. Rosenberg (Eds.) *Readings on the Sociology of Small Groups.* Englewood Cliffs, NJ: Prentice Hall, Inc.

13. Parsons, T. & Bales, R. F. (Eds.) (1955). *Family, Socialization, and Interactive Processes.* New York: The Free Press.

14. Marquis, D.G., Guetzkow, H. & Heyns, R.W. (1951) A SocialPsychological Study of the Decision Making Conference. In H. Guetzkow (Ed.) *Groups, Leadership and Men.* Pittsburg, PA: Carnegie Press.

15. Stouffer, S. A. et al. (1949). *The American Soldier: Studies in SocialPsychologyin World War II.* Princeton, NJ: Princeton University Press.

16. Shils, E. A. (1950). Primary Groups in the American Army. In R.Merton and P. Lazarsfeld (Eds.). *Continuities in Social Research Studies in the Scope and Method of "The American Soldier."* Glencoe, Ill: Free Press.

17. Grinker, R. R. and Spiegel, J. P. (1945). *Men Under Stress.* Philadelphia, PA: Blakiston

18. Shils, E. A. & Janowitz, M. (1948). Cohesion and Disintegration in the Wehrmacht in World War II. *Public Opinion Quarterly,* 12.

19. Appel, J.W., Beebe, G.W., & Hilger, D.W. (1946). Comparative incidence of neuropsychiatric casualties in World War I and World War II. *American Journal of Psychiatry, 102,* 196-199.

20. Staff report. (1984, July). Glen Srodes, 79 dies, Chief of Staff of Hospital.

PittsburghPost Gazette. Pittsburgh, PA.

21. Holmes, R. (1985). *Acts of War: The behavior of men in battle*. New York: Free Press.

22. Rogers, C. (1970). *Carl Rogers on Encounter Groups*. New York: Harper and Row.

23. Marshall. S. L.A. (1947). *Men Against Fire: The problem of battle command in future war.* New York: William Morrow.

24. NTL Institute for Applied Behavioral Sciences. (2004). Our History. http://www.ntl.org/about-history.html

25. Hill, R. (1958) Generic features of families under stress. *SocialCasework*, Vol. XXXIX, Nos. 2 and 3.

26. Hoult, J., Rosen, A, Reynolds, I. (1984).Community oriented treatment compared to psychiatric hospital oriented treatment. *Social Science and Medicine*, 18, 1005-1010.

27. Stein, L.I., Test, M.A. (1980). Alternative to mental hospital treatment: Conceptual Model, treatment programme and clinical evaluation. *Archives of General Psychiatry*, 37, 392-397.

28. Everly, G.S., Jr. (1999). Emergency Mental Health: An Overview.*International Journal of Emergency Mental Health*, 1, 3-7.

29. Mitchell, J.T. (2004). Characteristics of Successful Early InterventionPrograms. *International Journal of Emergency Mental Health*, 6 (4), 175-184.

30. Roberts, A. R. (2005) Bridging the Past and Present to the Future of Crisis Intervention and Crisis Management. In A.R. Roberts (Ed.) *Crisis Intervention Handbook: Assessment, Treatment, Research*. New York: Oxford University Press.

31. Gibson, M. (2006). *Order From Chaos: Responding to Traumatic Events.* Bristol: UK, The Policy Press, University of Bristol.

32. Mitchell, J.T. and Everly, G.S., Jr. (2001). *Critical Incident Stress Management: Basic Group Crisis Interventions*. Ellicott City, MD: International Critical Incident Stress Foundation.

33. Richards, D.(2001). A field study of critical incident stress debriefing versus critical incident stress management. *Journal of Mental Health*, 10, 351-362.

34. Campfield, K. & Hills, A. (2001). Effect of timing of critical Incident Stress Debriefing (CISD) on posttraumatic symptoms. *Journal of Traumatic Stress*, 14, 327-340.

35. Deahl, M., Srinivasan, M., Jones, N., Thomas, J., Neblett, C., & Jolly, A. (2000). Preventing psychological trauma in soldiers. The role of opera-

tional stress training and psychological debriefing. *British Journal of Medical Psychology*, 73, 77-85.

36. Boscarino, J.A., Adams, R.E. & Figley, C.R. (2005). A ProspectiveCohort Study of the Effectiveness of Employer-Sponsored Crisis Interventions after a Major Disaster. *International Journal of Emergency Mental Health*, 7(1), 31-44.

37. Mitchell, S.G. & Mitchell, J.T. (2006). Caplan, Community and Critical Incident Stress Management. *International Journal of Emergency Mental Health*, 8(1), 1-10.

38. Slaikeu, K.A. (1984). *Crisis intervention: A handbook for practice and research*. Boston, MA: Allyn and Bacon, Inc.

39. Yalom, I. D. and Leszcz, M. (2005). *The Theory and Practice of Group Psychotherapy*, 5th edition. New York: Basic Books.

40. Schein, L. A., Spitz, H. I., Burlingame, G.M., Muskin, P. R. &Vargo, S. (2006). *Psychological Effects of Catastrophic Disasters: Group Approaches to Treatment*. New York: Haworth Press.

41. Tindall, J. A. & Gray, H. D. (1985). *Peer Counseling*. Muncie, IN: Accelerated Development, Inc.

42. Brown, W. F. (1974). Effectiveness of paraprofessionals: The evidence. *Personnel and Guidance Journal*, 53(4), 257-264.

43. Fuhriman, A., & Burlingame, G. M. (1994). *Handbook of group psychotherapy: An empirical and clinical synthesis*. New York: John Wiley & Sons.

44. Burlingame, G. M., Fuhriman, A., & Mosier, J. (2003). The differential effectiveness of group psychotherapy: A meta-analytic perspective. *Group Dynamics: Theory, Research and Practice*, 7(1), 3-12.

45. McRoberts, C. Burlingame, G.M., & Hoag, M. J. (1998). Comparativeefficacy of individual and group psychotherapy: A meta-analytic perspective. *Group Dynamics: Theory, Research and Practice*, 2, 101-117.

46. Kyrouz, E. M., Humphreys, K. Loomis, C. (2002). A review of researchon the effectiveness of self-help mutual aid groups. In B. J. White and E. J. Madara (Eds.). *Self-Help Group Sourcebook: Your Guide to Community and Online Support Groups*. Cedar Knolls, NJ: American Self-Help Clearinghouse / Saint Clares Health Services.

47. Yalom, I. D. and Leszcz, M. (2005). *The Theory and Practice of Group Psychotherapy*, 5th edition. New York: Basic Books, p. 232.

48. Foy, D., Glynn, S., Schnurr, P. P., Jankowski, M. K., Wattenbgurg, M., Marmar, C. & Gusman, F. D. (2000). Group therapy. In E. B. Foa, T. M. Keane, and M.J. Friedman (Eds.), *Effective Treatments for PTSD*. New

York: Guilford Press, pp. 155-175.

49. Alexander, P. C., Neimeyer, R. A., Follette, V. M., Moore, M. K., & Harter, S. (1989). A comparison of group treatments of women sexually abused as children. *Journal of Consulting and Clinical Psychology*, 57, 479-483.

50. Chemtob, C. M. Nakashima, J. P., & Hamada, R. S. (2002). Psychosocial intervention for postdisaster trauma symptoms in elementary school children: A controlled community field study. *Archives of Pediatrics and Adolescent Medicine*, 156, 211-216.

51. Stalker, C. A. & Fry, R. (1999). A comparison of short-term group and individual therapy for sexually abused women. *Canadian journal of Psychiatry*, 44, 168-174.52. Stein, B. D., Jaycox, L.H., Kataoka, S. H., Wong, M., Tu,W. , Elliott, M. N. & Fink, A. (2003). A mental health intervention for schoolchildren exposed to violence: A randomized controlled trial. *Journal of thje American Medical Association*, 290, 603-611.

53. Zlotnick, C. Shea, M. T., Rosen, K. H., Simpson, E. Mulrenin, K., Begin, A., & Pearlstein, T. (1997). An affect-management group for woman with posttraumatic stress disorder and histories of childhood sexual abuse. *Journal of Traumatic Stress*, 10, 425-436.

54. Page, A. & Hooke, G. (2003). Outcomes for depressed and anxious inpatients discharged before and after group Cognitive Behaviour Therapy: A naturalistic comparison. *Journal of Nervous and Mental Disease*, 191, 653-659.

55. Reif, W., Trenkamp, S., Auer, C. & Fichter, (2000). Cognitive-Behaviour in panic disorder and comorbid major depression. *Psychotherapy and Psychosomatics*, 69, 70-78.

56. Longabaugh, R., Wirtz, P. Zweben, A., & Stout, R. (1998). Network support for drinking, Alcoholics Anonymous and long-term matching effects. *Addiction*, 93, 1313-1333.

57. Morgenstern, J., Labouvie, E., McCrady, B., Kahler, C., & Frey, R. (1997). Affiliation with Alcoholics Anonymous after treatment: A study of its therapeutic effects and mechanisms of action. *Journal of Consulting and Clinical Psychology*, 56, 768-777.

58. Walsh, D. C., Hingson, R.W., Merrigan, D. M., et al. (1991). A Randomized Trial of Treatment options for Alcohol-Abusing Workers. *New England Journal of Medicine*, 325 (11), 775-782.

59. McAuliffe, W. E. (1990). A Randomized Controlled Trial of Recovery Training and Self-Help for Opiod Addicts in New England and HongKong. *Journal of Psychoactive Drugs*, 22(2), 197-209.

60. Jason, L. A., Gruder, C. I., et al. (1987). Work site Group Meetings and the Effectiveness of a Televised Smoking Cessation Intervention. *American*

Journal of Community Psychology, 15, 57-77.

61. Caserta, M.S. & Lund, D. A. (1993). Intrapersonal Resources and the Effectiveness of Self-Help Groups for Bereaved Older Adults. *Gerontologist,* 33(5), 619-629.

62. Marmar, C. R., Horowitz, M. J. et al. (1988). A controlled Trial of Brief Psychotherapy and Mutual-Help Group Treatment of Conjugal Bereavement. *American Journal of Psychiatry,* 145(2), 203-209.

63. Videka-Sherman, L. & Lieberman, M. (1985). The Effects of Self-Help and Psychotherapy Intervention on Child Loss: The limits of Recovery. *American Journal of Orthopsychiatry* 55(1), 70-82.

64. Spiegel, D., Bloom, J. R., Kraemer, H. C. & Gottheil, E. (1989). Effects of psychosocial treatment on survival of patients with metastatic breast cancer. *The Lancet,* October 14, 888-891.

65. Dunham, P. J., Hurshman, A., Litwin, E., Gusella, J., Ellsworth, C. &Dodd, P.W. D. (1998) Computer-Mediated Social Support: Single Young Mothers as A Model System. *American Journal of Community Psychology,* 26, 281-306.

66. Walton, F. (2001). Combining abuse and neglect investigations with intensive family preservation services: An innovative approach to protecting children. *Research on Social Work Practice,* 11, 627-644.

67. Peterson, G., Abrams, D. B. et al. (1985). Professional versus self-help weight loss at the worksite: The challenge of making a public health impact. *Behavior Therapy, 16, 213-222.*

68. Kurtz, L. F. (1988). Mutual aid for affective disorders: The manic depressive and depressive association. *American Journal of Orthopsychiatry,* 58(1), 152-155.

69. Davies, D.R., Burlingame, G.M, & Layne, C.M. (2006). Integrating small-Group Process Principles into Trauma-Focused Group Psychotherapy: What Should a Group Trauma Therapist Know? In L. A. Schein, H. I. Spitz, G. M. Burlingame and P. R. Muskin (Eds). PsychologicalEffects of Catastrophic Disasters: Group Approaches to *Treatment.* New York: The Haworth Press, p. 388.

70. Yalom, I. D. and Leszcz, M. (2005). *The Theory and Practice of Group Psychotherapy, 5ᵗʰ edition.* New York: Basic Books, p. 102.

Chapter 5

Groups: The Operators' Manual

"All too often, group process is actually ignored and /or viewed as an interruption to the didactic presentation... To use the group medium effectively and to maximize the learning opportunities, the leader must be attuned to the movement and stirring within the group." *(1992, p. 241- 243)*[4]

~ Mark F. Ettin - *clinical psychologist, certified group psychotherapist, Adjunct Medical School Professor, and private practitioner. He is the inaugural recipient (1996) of the American Group Psychotherapy Foundation's award for excellence in psychodynamic group theory.*

INTRODUCTION

A group is an interactive system. Within the system are several interrelated components. The three main components discussed in this chapter are: 1) Group dynamics, 2) Group transactions, and 3) External Influences.

Group dynamics: The first component of the interactive system is **group dynamics. This is a set of relatively stable, yet somewhat fluid and complex internal relationships that have developed during the life of the group.** Some group specialists describe group dynamics synonymously with the term *group processes.* Other group experts convey subtle differences between the two terms and use them in different ways. To avoid confusion, **the two terms, group dynamics and group processes, will be used synonymously throughout this book.**

Group transactions: The second component of a group interactive system is group transactions. This term is simply a term of convenience for this particular publication. It is not likely that it will be found in other group-related publications. *This term, **group transactions, refers to the activities of the group members in accomplishing group goals**.* The most important transactions in a group are communication, decision making, problem solving, and the personal influence of individuals upon the other group members.

In a crisis situation, when an external crisis response team comes in to assist an existing homogeneous group, the established relationships (*dynamics or processes*) within the group and the manner in which the members communicate with each other and work together (*transactions*) will have considerable bearing on the suitability and effectiveness of the third component in a group interactive system – *external influences.*[1]

External influences are any forces or pressures from outside a group, that cause the group to react. There can be many types of external influences. Contact with individuals or other groups, authorities, legal systems, societal norms, customers, traumatic events, and the general population are but a few of the external influences on groups.

Since this book is about group crisis support, the discussion from here on will focus on the *external influence* of the crisis team's *group leadership skills*. The existing group dynamics and transactions will influence crisis team leadership functions and the selection of crisis interventions to match the group's needs. Group leadership skills may, likewise, have a limited influence the group's transactions, and, to a lesser extent, the group's dynamics.

The most effective crisis teams are properly trained and familiar with the literature on group work. However, the amount of literature available in the group field is immense. Therefore, only a tiny portion of its most pertinent elements can be addressed in this book.

By the conclusion of the chapter, the reader should be clear about the key internal group dynamics or processes, as well as the transactions and the effects of the crisis team's group leadership skills. **A well-trained, educated, and skillful crisis team can help to re-establish *group cohesiveness* and *maximum levels of performance* in primary groups dealing with an exposure to a critical incident.** Guidelines in this book may help crisis teams avoid some of the potential pitfalls of group work.

GOALS of GROUP CRISIS SUPPORT

It is extremely important, before engaging in any group crisis support services, that the response team be very clear about the aims of group crisis support. No attempt is made in group crisis support to cure any physical disease or mental disorder; nor is any attempt made to alter the existing long-standing group dynamics within a group. A failure to accept the primary goals and the limitations of group crisis support services may be the cause of crisis team frustration and a failed stress management mission.

Group work in crisis situations should focus on **three main goals:**
1) the mitigation of the impact of a critical incident, **2) the facilitation of recovery** from traumatic experience, as well as the restoration of adaptive group functions, and **3) the detection of individual** members from within the group **who might benefit from additional support services** or perhaps a referral for professional care if that is necessary.

Objectives beyond the above three primary goals, such as personality change, the prevention of all post-traumatic reactions, or alterations in group dynamics, are unrealistic and outside the scope of group crisis intervention. **Group crisis intervention is only a support process, not therapy.** [2]

IMPORTANT NOTE!
The group crisis *support services* described in this book should NEVER be construed to be any form of psychotherapy nor a substitute for psychotherapy. They are support services only.

GROUP DYNAMICS
Group dynamics (group processes) refers to the internal forces, influences, relationships, conflicts, and behaviors between the group members. Group dynamics develop within the group over the course of its life and define how the group formed and configured itself as it developed. The dynamics explained in these pages are found in almost any group.

More than 70 years of studies on group interactions support our current knowledge of group dynamics.[3-6] Research indicates that there are predictable interrelationships and behaviors that should be expected in groups. Group dynamics exist whether or not a crisis situation occurs, but they may be dampened or magnified in the midst of crises. The influence of group dynamics is potentially quite powerful during a crisis and may cause surprising disruptions in group support sessions. In some cases, group dynamics may cause a group or some of its members to resist or reject group support entirely. It is essential, therefore, that crisis response team members recognize and adapt to the group interrelationships that were present in the group long before the critical incident that triggered a crisis team response.[6,7]

Group dynamics can change slowly over time. It is usually not possible to substantially alter the core dynamics of a group during the short time frames associated with crisis intervention services. Modifications in the dynamics within a group take both a considerable amount of time and a potent stimulus driving the changes. Changes in group dynamics, therefore, should certainly **not** be the aim of a crisis response team when providing group crisis support.

Some of the key group dynamics are listed in table 5.1. The table also provides questions for the crisis response team to keep in mind while preparing to provide group crisis intervention. The crisis intervention team members might actually ask some of these questions while meeting with group members. Other questions may be answered indirectly as the crisis team members gather information about the group while making their assessment prior to the group session. Some questions are not actually answered, but they may help the crisis team be more alert to potential group processes.

It is not essential that all the questions in table 5.1 be answered, but being aware of both the questions and the dynamics can prepare the crisis team to deal with a *complex interactive group system*. Knowledge of the nature of the group and its internal dynamics can help the team to avoid disrupting or challenging the normal processes within a group. In other words, crisis team members should avoid the psychological equivalent of "stepping on someone's toes." It is far better to work carefully with existing dynamics within a group than to haphazardly approach a group as if these dynamics were not present. When in doubt, always assume that a number of group dynamics are constantly at work within every group.[5, 6]

Although there is a risk of oversimplification, *the term **group dynamics** or **group processes** in this book is used primarily to describe the relationships between group members that were established well before a crisis event occurred and before meeting the crisis response team.* A group, in other words, brings its own set of group dynamics into a crisis intervention situation. Those dynamics will be operating at all times, even when they are not obvious. They may either help the group crisis intervention process, be neutral to it, or they may impair the ability of a crisis team to provide group crisis support.[2, 6, 7]

Table 5.1.
Common Group Dynamics
(Pre-existing nature and structure of the group)

- **Group composition**. Who are the members? Is the group newly formed or has it been operational for a long time? Are they all original group members or have there been changes? Are there several new members in the group? Are the training and experience levels about the same or very different?

- **Group structure**. How is the group organized? Is there a hierarchy in the group? Does the primary group exist within a larger secondary group, such as a school or an army?

- **Group norms**. What are the formal and informal rules that guide the group member behaviors? Are there group taboos or topics to be avoided?

- **Group culture**. What is the history and background of the group and what kinds of accomplishments have been achieved? What are approved behaviors for the group? What is likely to be rejected in the group? Is it all right for the group to accept outside support? Does the group allow self-disclosure among its members? Does the group allow self-disclosure to outsiders?

- **Group leadership (internal)**. What kind of leadership exists within the group (democratic, autocratic, or laissez faire)? What leadership styles exist within the larger organization if there is one? Who has power in the group? Who has appointed power? Who has perceived power?

- **Group task**. Why does this group exist? What functions or tasks does the group perform?

- **Group member roles**. What roles do the various group members perform in the group? What is expected of each of the group members?

- **Group cohesiveness**. How closely bonded are the group members? How well do they get along? Do the members seem to like one another? How do they view their group? How supportive are they of one another? Do members function for self benefit or for the benefit of the group? Do people personally identify with being part of the group?

- **Group conflict?** What are the sources of conflict in the group? Who does not seem to get along with others? Who appears isolated from the other group members?

- **Group climate**. Is there respect and appreciation for the members of the group? Is the atmosphere of the group a positive one or is it negative? Are people's talents recognized? Are people given credit for what they achieve? [6,7]

GROUP TRANSACTIONS

Group transactions are defined as the procedures that groups use to communicate, assess and analyze issues, evaluate options, pool ideas, solve problems, manage conflicts, make decisions, and achieve outcomes. Group transactions are the activities by which a group does its work and accomplishes its goals. Group transactions go on between the group members themselves and between the group and external influences, such as the crisis team providing support. Remember, the dynamics described earlier and portrayed in table 5.1 are not going to disappear while a crisis team is engaged in activities intended to help the group deal with a crisis response. Group dynamics will influence virtually every aspect of the internal group transactions and the contacts with the crisis team.[7-13]

Table 5.2.

Transactions within Crisis Intervention Groups
(How groups communicate and achieve their goals)

- Establishing safety and security
- Introduction of participants
- Communication
- Presentation of issues
- Analysis / interpretation
- Proposals
- Counterproposals
- Conflict resolution
- Problem solving
- Choosing best options
- Finding consensus
- Decision making
- Development of a plan
- Handling the unexpected challenges
- Managing disappointments and frustrations
- Adapting to external forces
- Dealing with group duress
- Caring for distressed individual members
- Assignment of tasks to group members
- Closure of the meeting and implementation of results

CRISIS TEAM GROUP LEADER SKILLS

A crisis response team requires many group leadership skills. The team has to be aware of the dynamics that exist in the group and it has to facilitate a variety of group transactions to help bring the distress in the group under control. The crisis team must first establish a safe environment for the group and it must choose the best tactics or *group leadership skills* to enhance the potential that the group crisis support process will be successful. Crisis response teams should remember that a group has its own "personality" just as individuals have their own individual personality. The sum of all the behaviors, feelings, and interactions of the group members is, by far, larger than each of the individuals in the group.

All of the group dynamics, transactions, and the need for a wide range of group leadership skills on the part of the crisis team make group crisis intervention considerably more complex than individual crisis intervention. All complex tasks demand training and practice, and group crisis intervention is no exception. Proper training, practice, and supervision is crucial to the mitigation of traumatic stress and a return of the group members to a high level of unit cohesion and maximal unit performance.[2, 3, 6, 7, 9]

Table 5.3 lists many of the group-leadership skills that are required of crisis team members when they are dealing with distressed or traumatized groups.

Group research indicates that there are certain group leader guidelines that can maximize the additive positive effects of group dynamics and group transactions.[3]

The first crisis intervention guideline for use in almost all groups is to pay attention to **interpersonal feedback**. Interpersonal feedback represents the informative and sometimes corrective communications shared between group members.[14] A crisis response team should be aware that internal communications between group members will continue even in the midst of a structured group crisis intervention process. Sometimes those comments are strictly between one group member and another. As long as the communications between the group members do not become disruptive, they should be allowed. For instance, a whisper between group members is usually fine in a supportive crisis group. The crisis team leader would be wise to let those whispers pass without comment.

Sometimes group members comment out loud and attempt to correct another group member's misinterpretation of the traumatic experience. For example, if a person openly blames himself for a mistake that produced negative consequences, several members of the group may react to the self-blaming individual and inform him or her that the entire group was involved in the

Table 5.3.

Group Leadership Skills - External Influences

(What the crisis team brings to the group)

- Establish a safe environment for the group
- Establish an adequate structure for the group
- Motivate group members
- Encourage group member participation
- Explore pertinent issues
- Respond actively
- Demonstrate leadership
- Maintain an atmosphere of respect for the group members
- Use accurate empathy with group members
- Accept and validate emotions
- Manage conflict between group members
- Encourage appropriate self disclosure
- Help group members to own their own reactions by speaking about their roles and reactions in the traumatic event
- Carefully use challenging skills (mild confrontation) when required in a group to correct inaccurate perceptions
- Call for feedback from group members to help a member who is "stuck"
- Provide feedback from a crisis team perspective
- Identify group member strengths
- Provide information and education on issues of traumatic stress
- Provide concrete information and avoid abstract or theoretical information
- Summarize the group meeting
- Provide final directives
- Arrange for follow-up services
- Provide closure to the meeting [2, 3, 6, 7, 22]

same action and that no one person can accept all the responsibility for the group's decisions or activities.

At other times, the message from one group member might be helpful for all to hear, but only a portion of the group has heard the comment. It is as if the person were "thinking out loud" and only the nearby people hear the remark. The comments of one group member can be brought out to the whole group. In a situation like this, a crisis team member can incorporate the comment into the entire group discussion by saying something, such as, "I just heard you make an excellent comment that I think is important for all of the members to hear; but, I don't think they all heard you. Would you mind repeating that important comment for the benefit of everyone?" If the person is hesitant to repeat the comment, ask if it would be alright if you were to summarize the comment for the benefit of the others.

The second guideline for work in groups is to be aware of the important role of **self-disclosure**.[15] It is generally a positive activity in a group when individuals open up and inform the other group members about their personal reactions and concerns. The crisis intervention team leading the session must be skillful in meeting the challenges that arise as a group engages in its transactions. Too much self-disclosure, especially in the earliest stages of a group crisis intervention, can generate anxiety in the other group members. On the other hand, too little self-disclosure also generates considerable anxiety and mistrust in the other group members.

A balance is necessary; the crisis team has to work hard to achieve that balance.[3, 7] When self-disclosure is taking place, it should be gradual and reciprocal.[15, 16] That is why a Critical Incident Stress Debriefing (CISD; see Chapter 11) begins with the cognitive aspects of the event, then moves toward the thoughts the group members may have (less intense disclosure), eventually moving to the worst aspects of the event (more intense disclosure).[2] Everyone is given an opportunity in the fact phase and the thought phase to express themselves if they wish. That makes the disclosure reciprocal and graduated.[15]

The third guideline in groups is to aim at **universality** in the group transactions. The interpersonal feedback and the self-disclosure, when combined in the interactive environment of a crisis intervention group, may establish a beneficial atmosphere. Individual group members realize that they are not alone in their reactions to a traumatic event. They feel more normal regarding their experiences and they learn coping methods from each other.[3, 15] During either a defusing or a Critical Incident Stress Debriefing, for example, the teaching phase is used to solidify some of the information the group members have gained from each other.[2]

The fourth general guideline for group transaction in a crisis intervention is to generate *role flexibility* within the group. The group members may receive help at certain times and give it at others. In order to achieve role flexibility, the crisis team needs to keep the group focused on the "here and now" discussions in the group.[3, 15] The team leading a group crisis intervention must work to help the participants to be both recipients and contributors of information and assistance.[2, 7] Even simple comments from group leaders can encourage role flexibility in a group. For example, it may be helpful to say, "You may find, in a meeting like this, that something one person says, which might seem unimportant, may be quite helpful to someone else in the group".

The fifth guideline for managing transactions in groups is to establish a *structure* for the group meeting. Structure creates a "safe" environment within the group and allows a controlled flow of information and self disclosure.[3] There is a long history of literature that emphasizes both the necessity and the benefits of providing structure in groups.[16] As far back as 1974 group process authors warned that a "lack of structure…feeds clients' distortions, interpersonal fears and subjective distress…."[17] A structure that permits all the members of a group to contribute a small piece to the discussion enhances a sense of commonality in the group.[18] Groups with appropriate structure tend to be fairly cohesive; they also appear to be more confident in their self disclosure.[19]

IMPORTANT NOTE:

Having expertise in individual support processes by no means guarantees that a person will be able to provide services in a group setting. Individual processes and, likewise, group-specific processes cannot easily be transferred from one approach to the other. Different skills are required in each modality.[20, 21]

GENERAL GROUP LEADER GUIDELINES for CRISIS GROUPS

It is important that anyone providing group crisis support, whether in large groups or in small, observes general guidelines for group intervention. These guidelines reduce the risk of harm to the group members and improve the crisis team's ability to effectively facilitate the group.

- Crisis team members must be *properly trained* to handle a group.

- Crisis team members should be *supervised* by a mental health professional.

- Crisis team members should be *familiar with the literature* on reactions to critical incidents.

- The crisis team should make *participants as comfortable as possible.*

- The crisis team should provide for *physical necessities and group security* as much as possible.

- A crisis team should foster social support by assuring that groups are as *homogeneous as possible.*

- A crisis group should help to *decrease a sense of isolation in its members.*

- *The provision of information is vital* in all crisis groups whether they be homogeneous (similar in membership) or heterogeneous (mixed membership). Depending on the circumstances, different types and amounts of information may be necessary for the different types of groups.

- The crisis group should *provide an opportunity to rebuild trust* among the members of the group.

- Even *large groups should be as homogeneous as possible,* although more heterogeneity is tolerated in large groups. The more heterogeneous a group is, the more the leaders must focus on information and not on discussion of affective (emotional) material.

- Since structure is an "antidote" to chaos, crisis groups should *provide structure.*

- Crisis groups should always be *a source of information, education, guidance, and direction* for the group members.

- Crisis team leaders should provide *comfort, consolation, and support.*

- When appropriate, crisis groups should *allow emotional ventilation* in a setting that is safe and has an accepting and encouraging atmosphere.

- The crisis team should *validate the reactions* to the traumatic experience and *help the members gain insight* into how the event has impacted their own view of the world.

- Crisis teams should help the group members with *symptom management.*

- A group crisis support service *aims at mitigating the impact of an event, facilitating the recovery process, and identifying individuals who may need additional support.*

- A group crisis support process should *promote healthy behaviors and mental health.*

- A group crisis support should *facilitate access to additional care* if it is required.

- The crisis team should *triage, follow-up, and refer* individual members of the group as necessary to professional resources or support networks.[22-29]

Figure 5.1 describes the interrelationship between group dynamics, group processes, and the team's crisis intervention skills and techniques described in the preceding sections.

SUMMARY

This chapter covered four important issues. First, it addressed *group dynamics.* Those are the group structure and interaction issues that have long been established in the group. The dynamics of a particular group define the essence of group, its core structure, and the relationships between its members. Second, this chapter discussed *group transactions.* How a group communicates and works among its members and between the group and the outside world is what group transactions are all about. The third important issue is the *group leader skills* brought in by a crisis response team. These skills relate to how a group crisis support meeting is conducted. The fourth major issue discussed in this chapter is *a set of general helpful guidelines* for managing crisis support groups.

All four major issues are interwoven during a group crisis support session. Obviously, that can make a group intervention a somewhat complex interaction. Research, however, indicates several advantages to group intervention and points out directions for team members to follow to keep group crisis support manageable.

The next chapter aims at expanding the knowledge base behind the basic group theory and the principles of group management that have been described in the previous chapters.

Figure 5.1.

Combinations of: 1) group dynamics, 2) group transactions and 3) team member group leadership skills make group support a complex interaction

Group Dynamics:

The nature and structure of the group combined with its cohesiveness, internal leadership, norms, and individual member characteristics.

{The group enters a group crisis intervention with all of these already in place}

+

Group Transactions:

Communications and interactions between group members and between group members and the crisis team. These may also exist before the crisis.

+

Crisis Team Group Leadership Skills:

These are the procedures that the team initiates and controls during the group crisis intervention session. It includes attending, guiding, questioning, directing, motivating, facilitating, confronting, acknowledging, validating, reassuring, and supporting the group members.

=

Group Interactive System

REFERENCES - Chapter 5

1. Bales, R. F. (1970). Interaction Process Analysis. In T. M. Mills & S. Rosenberg (Eds.) *Readings on the sociology of small groups.* Englewood Cliffs, NJ: Prentice Hall.

2. Mitchell, J.T. & Everly, G.S., Jr., (2001). *Critical Incident Stress* Debriefing: An operations manual for CISD, Defusing and other *group crisis intervention services, Third Edition.* Ellicott City, MD: Chevron.

3. Davies, D.R., Burlingame, G.M, & Layne, C.M. (2006). Integrating small-Group Process Principles into Trauma-Focused Group Psychotherapy: What Should a Group Trauma Therapist Know? In L. A. Schein, H. I. Spitz, G. M. Burlingame and P. R. Muskin (Eds). *Psychological Effects of Catastrophic Disasters: Group Approaches to Treatment.* New York: The Haworth Press, 385-423.

4. Ettin, M. F. (1992). *Foundations and applications of group psychotherapy: A sphere of influence.* Needham Heights, MA: Allyn and Bacon, p.243.

5. Olmstead, M.S. Hare, A. P. (1978). *The Small Group, 2ⁿᵈ edition.* New York: Random House.

6. Yalom, I. D. and Leszcz, M. (2005). *The Theory and Practice of Group Psychotherapy, 5ᵗʰ edition.* New York: Basic Books.

7. Dyregrov, A. (2003). *Psychological Debriefing: A leader's guide for*small group crisis intervention. Ellicott City, MD: Chevron Publishing Corporation.

8. Kyrouz, E. M., Humphreys, K. Loomis, C. (2002). A review of research on the effectiveness of self-help mutual aid groups. In B. J. White and E. J. Madara (Eds.). *Self-Help Group Sourcebook: Your Guide to Community and Online Support Groups.* Cedar Knolls, NJ: American Self-Help Clearinghouse / Saint Clares Health Services.

9. Schein, L. A., Spitz, H. I., Burlingame, G.M., Muskin, P. R. &Vargo, S. (Eds.) (2006). *Psychological Effects of Catastrophic Disasters: Group Approaches to Treatment.* New York: Haworth Press.

10. Foy, D.W., Glynn, S.M., Schnurr, P. P., Jankowski, M.K., Wattenberg, M. S., Weiss, D. S., Marmar, C. R. & Gusman, F. D. (2000). Group Therapy. In E. Foa, T. Keane & M. Friedman EDS.) *Effective* treatments for PTSD: Practice guidelines from the International *Society for Traumatic Stress Studies.* New York: Guilford Press, pp. 155-175, 336-338.

11. Roberts, A. & Everly, G. S., Jr. (2006). A Merta-Analysis of 36 Crisis Intervention Studies. *Brief Treatment and Crisis Intervention,*6 (1), 10-21.

12. Burlingame, G. M., MacKenzie, K. R., & Strauss, B. (2004). *Evidence-based group treatment: matching models with disorder and patients.* Washington, DC: American Psychological Association.

13. Burlingame, G.M., Mackenzie, K.R. & Strauss, B. (2003). Small group treatment: Evidence for Effectiveness and mechanisms of change. In M. Lambert, A.E. Bergin & S.L. Garfield (Eds.) *Handbook of Psychotherapy and behavior change,* 5th edition. New York: John Wiley and Sons, 647-696.

14. Fuhriman, A. & Burlingame, G. M. (1990). Consistency of matter: A comparative analysis of individual and group process variables. *The Counseling Psychologist,* 18, 7-63.

15. Stockton, R. & Moran, D.K. (1982). Review and perspective of critical dimensions in therapeutic small group research. In G. M. Gazda (Ed.), *Basic approaches to group psychotherapy.* Springfiled, IL: Thomas.

16. Stockton, R., Rohde, R. I. & Haughey, J. (1992). The effects of structured group exercises on cohesion, engagement, avoidance and conflict. *Small Group Research,* 23, 155-168.

17. Bednar, R. L., Melnick, J., & Kaul, T.J. (1974). Risk, responsibility, and structure: A conceptual framework for initiating group counseling and psychotherapy. *Journal of Counseling Psychology,* 21, 31-37.

18. Layne, C. M., Saltzman, W. R., Steinberg, A. S. & Pynoos, R. S. (2003). *Trauma/ grief-focused group psychotherapy for adolescents.* Los Angeles, CA: national Center for Child Traumatic Stress.

19. Dies, R. R. (1994). Therapist variable in group psychotherapy research. In A. Fuhriman & G. M. Burlingame (Eds.), *Handbook of group psychotherapy: An empirical and clinical synthesis.* New York: Wiley, 114-154.

20. Block, S., & Crouch, E. (1985). *Therapeutic factors in group psychotherapy.* London: Oxford University Press.

21. Wilfley, D. E., Frank, M. A., Welch, R., Spurell, E. B. & Rounsaville, B. J. (1998). Adapting interpersonal psychotherapy to a group format (IPT-G) for binge eating disorder: Toward a model for adapting empirically supported treatments. *Psychotherapy Research,* 8, 379-391.

22. Egan, G. (1976). *Interpersonal Living: A skills / contract approach to Human-relations training in groups.* Monterey, CA: Brooks/ Cole Publishing Company.

23. Kaul , T. J. & Bednar, R. L. (1994). Pretraining and structure: Parallel lines yet to meet. In A. Fuhriman and G. M. Burlingame (Eds.) Handbook of group psychotherapy: An empirical and clinical *synthesis.* New York: Wiley, p. 161.

24. Burlingame, G. M., Fuhriman, A. & Johnson, J. E. (2002). Cohesion in group psychotherapy. In J. Norcross (Ed.), *Psychotherapy relationships that work*. New York: Oxford University Press, 71-88.

25. Janoff-Bulman, R. (1992). *Shattered assumptions: Toward a new psychology of trauma*. New York: Free Press.

26. Everly, G. S, Jr., Phillips, S. B., Kane, D. & Feldman, D. (2006). Introduction to and overview of Group Psychological First Aid. *Brief Treatment and Crisis Intervention*, 6, 130-136.

27. Raphael, B. (1986). *When Disaster Strikes*. New York: Basic Books.

28. Ulman, K. H. (2004). Group interventions for treatment of trauma in adults. In B. J. Buchele & H. I. Spitz (Eds.), *Group interventions for treatment of psychological trauma*. New York: American Group Psychotherapy Association.

29. VandenBos, G., Editor in Chief. (2007). *APA Dictionary of Psychology*. Washington, DC: American Psychological Association.

Chapter 6

A Deeper Understanding of Groups

*"Knowledge has to be improved, challenged, and
increased constantly, or it vanishes."*
~ Peter Ferdinand Drucker *(1909–2005). Austrian born
author of management literature and Professor of Management
at New York University*

INTRODUCTION

A recent 20-year, longitudinal study on soldiers who had received front line crisis support services on or near the battlefield indicates that even small, well-managed crisis intervention procedures had long lasting positive effects. Two decades after their combat experiences, soldiers who received support services at or near the front lines of the battle had fewer or less severe posttraumatic and psychiatric symptoms, suffered less from loneliness, and functioned better socially than soldiers who had not received frontline support. Furthermore, the more interventions that were used in combination, the greater were the positive effects.[1] Group research literature indicates many similar positive findings. Positive outcomes in groups were, more often than not, dependent on knowledgeable and skillful group facilitators.[2-10]

Clearly, too much is at stake for group crisis support personnel to limit their knowledge of groups. The more they know of the functions and behaviors associated with group support, the more effective will be their interventions.

This chapter aims to strengthen the foundations for group support that have been established in previous chapters. In addition, this chapter should help to broaden the reader's knowledge of groups and group support. Ultimately, the goal of this chapter is assure that group crisis support personnel are as fully informed as possible to take on the responsibilities of providing a broad range of group crisis support services.

ACTIVE FACTORS in GROUP INTRERVENTIONS

It is difficult to say with absolute certainty why group support tends to have positive effects on the group members. The research regarding the benefits of group intervention, however, is strongly and persistently positive with many types of groups and with many different human problems.[5, 8, 9-11] More than likely, the positive effects of group intervention are associated with combinations of numerous factors, including the group dynamics, group transactions, and group leader skills described in the previous chapter.

Group researches have identified several important factors that are considered the main "active factors" in group support. They are

- the theoretical framework,

- member characteristics,

- leadership characteristics,

- small group processes, and

- group structure.

A little more detail on these five active factors in group support services follows below.

Theoretical framework. A theoretical framework serves as the rationale or foundation for specific group interventions. There are many theoretical frameworks. Psychodynamic, cognitive-behavioral, process, and educational group theories are examples of some of the main theoretical frameworks in group interventions. Each theoretical framework has been developed with specific purposes in mind.

- **In groups based on psychodynamic theory**, a professionally trained group psychotherapist helps the group interpret possible unconscious motives that may have influenced the behaviors of the group members. The psychodynamic approach to group work emphasizes emotions rather than thought processes. The emphasis is on tracing group behaviors to their origins. The leader encourages the clients in the group to take more responsibility for their own behaviors and to help the other group members to take responsibility for themselves. The group dynamics that occur during a group meeting are carefully followed by the group leader, who often encourages the group members to discuss both the behaviors of individuals within the group and the group interactions among the various members. Eventually the psychodynamic therapist utilizes the group to guide the group members toward individual life changes.[12-13]

- **When a cognitive-behavioral theoretical framework is selected** for group work, the psychotherapist group leader focuses on enhancing, informing, restructuring, or altering knowledge, perceptions, reasoning, and judgment in order to modify human behaviors. Certain positive thoughts that lead to healthy behaviors within the group are encouraged. On the other hand, flawed thinking, that may lead to less than desirable behaviors, is challenged within the group. Therapists who utilize this theoretical framework must be trained in cognitive-behavioral therapy.[14]

- **A group based on the process theoretical framework** deals with the attitudes, perceptions, and emotions that exist between the individual members of the group and the other group members. Leaders in such groups are not always mental health professionals. Sometimes, these groups are led by teams of specially trained peer support personnel who work together with and are guided by a mental health professional. A team usually focuses on the attitudes, perceptions, and emotions of the group members toward the traumatic event they encountered. Process group leaders inquire about the actions of the group members during the traumatic event and their thoughts, attitudes, and reactions to the experience. The opinions of every group member are valued and accepted. The right of group members to remain silent is always respected. Skillful leaders incorporate group members into the helping process whenever possible during the meeting. That is, all group members are viewed as potential support resources for their colleagues. This group framework is particularly helpful with peer-oriented traumatic stress groups, such as the defusing and the Critical Incident Stress Debriefing.[6, 15]

- **A group based on the educational theoretical framework** focuses on informing, educating, advising, and directing group members in an effort to influence beliefs or behaviors. There is less emphasis on the opinions and beliefs of other group members to influence positive changes in individual group members. It is expected, in such groups, that the group leaders will provide ample amounts of information from which the group members can draw their own conclusions. Again, the group leaders are not always mental health professionals. This theoretical framework is particularly common in large group interventions such as Post Operations Stress Information and Support services (demobilization) and Crisis Management Briefings.[15]

It might be assumed that different group theoretical frameworks would produce different results, but a recent literature review suggests that each theoretical framework has generated roughly equal positive results.[14] Some authors explain this equality of results by suggesting that the mere association and interactions between group members may be powerful enough to have some therapeutic effects, regardless of the type of group. [3]

Member characteristics. Are group members other-centered or self-centered? Do they hold similar or dissimilar beliefs and philosophy? Do they have similar backgrounds? Are the members rigid or flexible? Would the members be more conservative or liberal in their thinking process? Is the group homogeneous or heterogeneous? Groups that have members who are fairly similar to one another appear to be more supportive of their members and are perceived by one another to be more supportive and helpful.[6, 15-18]

Leadership characteristics. The least likeable leaders are the **autocrats.** Some people perceive them as being 'bossy.' They are credited, however, with elevated levels of group achievement because their demands are high and they push their personnel to achieve group goals.

The most likeable leaders have a **democratic** style. The group members feel that they have a say in important matters. A democratic style can encourage a group to function somewhere between moderate and very high levels of performance, depending on the relationship the leader establishes with the group. If a democratic style is taken to an extreme, however, group productivity will be impaired or blocked. The impairment occurs because the leader is so focused on what each and every group member thinks that decisions are constantly delayed or avoided altogether.

The least productive leaders, and often least respected, are those who lead with **a "laissez faire"** attitude. No one in the group knows what is expected of them and the group members often complain of a lack of leadership, a clear plan, or a set of achievable goals. The group is left to its own devices and, unless perceived leadership within the group takes over, the group cannot achieve its objectives. Laissez faire leaders are particularly unhelpful in a crisis situation.[19, 20]

Group dynamics and group transactions. Considerable discussion has already been presented in Chapter 5 on these two factors. They are such important factors in group work that they are mentioned here again. Group dynamics refer to the nature and structure of groups and the group transactions are the ways in which groups interrelate, communicate and carry out their functions. Clear and understandable group processes and agreed upon group transactions are fundamental to a high degree of group cohesion and performance.[21]

Group structure. This refers to how the group is organized. Who takes the lead roles in the group? Is power shared or tightly held by one person. Is leadership fixed or rotated? Are there single or multiple leadership levels within a group? Is there a possibility for the lower level personnel to communicate with the senior personnel?[3, 5, 6, 11, 14, 15]

(Please see Chapter 5 for more information on group dynamics, group transactions, and group leader skills.)

STRUCTURE, CONTENT, and GROUP PROCESS

Working to support a group in crisis takes a great deal of energy on the part of the crisis team. The ever-present dynamics of the group combined with the individual personalities of the group members will cause the group to have its own "personality." Add to this the important "active factors" of a crisis team's interventions, as well as the many group transactions that are involved in a group, and the crisis response team can easily feel overwhelmed.[3, 5, 10] Indeed, in some circumstances, group crisis support can be a complex interaction![21]

There are, however, some things at work within groups that can make group crisis support manageable and effective. A group intervention needs an operational structure to guide people through the distress that was generated by the critical incident. To enhance structure in groups, specific models have been developed, such as defusing, Crisis Management Briefing, and a variety of "debriefing" models, including the Critical Incident Stress Debriefing. The structure provided by appropriate applications of group crisis intervention models is enormously helpful to both the crisis team and to those who receive the group support. The majority of group crisis support personnel state that they find a model is a useful guideline that seems to carry the group process along. They report that their own anxieties and those of the group members decline as the group intervention proceeds.

Group crisis support models are not accidental occurrences; they have been developed upon the background of the very best of knowledge and research in crisis intervention, group intervention, community psychology, and peer support services. The structures provided by the group crisis support models in this book are empirically sound and deeply rooted in solid group theory and clearly defined practices that have evolved during the last 100 years. [2, 3, 5, 9 — 11, 13 – 21]

There is something else that may work to the advantage of the crisis team: the *homogeneity* of the group. The more homogeneous a group, the greater is the potential for a positive outcome in group crisis support. A homogeneous group is already a *primary group*. Primary groups are frequently enormously helpful to their members. The crisis team does not need to lead them through the steps required for the formation of a primary group. They are generally ready to support one another. Many group dynamics have already developed within the group and they can be used by a skilled crisis team to achieve the main crisis intervention goals: 1) mitigation of the stress response, 2) a facilitation of recovery and a restoration to adaptive functions, and 3) the identification of group members who may need more support.

Another issue to consider is the fact that the trauma that generated disruption in the group actually opens up opportunities for a crisis team. A trained, knowledgeable, and skillful crisis team, that is willing to hear the disturbing content of the traumatic experience, will be welcomed by many groups. The content of the crisis-related discussion generates activity in all of the common group transactions including structure, interpersonal feedback, self-disclosure, universality, and role flexibility (see Chapter 5).

It would be a serious mistake for a crisis support team to underestimate *the power of the group* itself. Some crisis management work in a crisis intervention group is performed by the crisis team, but **the group itself can be the most potent source of healing and recovery for the group members**. The group processes and transactions described in Chapter 5 are extremely important in the restoration of group health, unit cohesion, and unit performance. Interpersonal feedback and self- disclosure within a group, for example, play extraordinary roles in group member recovery. The crisis team only has the privilege of temporarily guiding a group during a period of acute distress. One review of a decade's studies on the effects of member-to-member feedback concluded "feedback from others is commonly accepted as a critical therapeutic factor in group treatment and is so widely held that we would be embarrassed to mention it to an audience of group leaders." [22 - 24]

REMEMBER!
Some crisis management work in a crisis intervention group is performed by the crisis team, but the group itself can be the most potent source of healing and recovery for the group members... The crisis team only has the privilege of temporarily guiding a group during a period of acute distress.

THERAPEUTIC FACTORS in GROUPS
Irvin Yalom, the grand master of group process, has identified eleven therapeutic factors in groups. They are

- Installation of hope
- Universality
- Imparting information
- Altruism
- The corrective feedback of the primary group
- Development and socializing techniques
- Imitative behavior
- Interpersonal learning
- Group cohesiveness
- Catharsis
- Existential factors[5] [(p.1)]

Yalom clearly points out that the items on the list are actually influenced by each other so they should not be considered as separate, isolated items. In several studies the items were *rank ordered by group participants from most helpful to the least helpful* for clients in a group. Here is the list again, but this time it is in a rank ordered format with some slight alterations based on group member perceptions.

- Learning about oneself from group members
- Catharsis
- Group cohesiveness
- Self understanding
- Interpersonal output
- Existential factors
- Universality
- Installation of hope
- Altruism
- Family reenactment
- Guidance
- Personal identification with other group members or group leaders.[5(p.88), 25]

Group crisis support leaders must be well aware of the therapeutic factors in groups because it is their job to incorporate or encourage as many of these therapeutic factors as possible in group work.[26, 27, 28]

DOMAINS

One final important issue as we approach the conclusion of this chapter is the issue of *domains* of discussion. **Domain refers to a category or sphere of influence.** *There are three main domains in human experience. One is physical, the second is cognitive, and the third is affective or emotional.* Although, to some degree or another, physical manifestations always accompany the cognitive and affective domains, this section will focus on the *cognitive and emotional domains.* Crisis response personnel must keep these domains in mind. They relate to the discussion of the traumatic content and to the reactions of the group members. They help to give the crisis support team a general "road map" for the type of content that will be heard (and sometimes observed) in a crisis group.

Cognitive domain content simply offers us the facts; it describes thinking processes.

Affective domain content tells us more about what group members are feeling. On occasion, someone will speak as if they are in the cognitive domain, but in reality they are relating to the affective domain. A person might say, for instance, that they are "fine," but bite their lip, clench their teeth, or punch a fist into a wall. The statement of "fine" (cognitive) is not what is really meant. The observed behaviors suggest that the person is caught up in an affective response. Crisis team members might ask a cognitive question and receive an affective answer. For example, "Can you briefly tell our team a little about the experience you had?" That is a cognitive question. If the answer comes back, "I was never so scared in my life!" it is an affective response.

Knowing the domain someone happens to be in helps a crisis team member to carefully and appropriately respond to the person. On the other hand, not knowing the person's domain may cause us to misinterpret the meaning of their comment and respond inappropriately to it. For example, if a person says, "I feel as if this is entirely my fault" (affective) and the crisis team responds with "The report does not suggest that the situation was caused by anybody" (cognitive), then the crisis team essentially has ignored the person's affective content. The crisis team member's response is not helpful. It would be more helpful if the crisis team member responded with something on the order of, "I hear you saying that and I am sure that is a painful feeling for you right now. Let's keep that in mind and see if something comes up in this meeting that helps you to see the circumstances a little differently. You might also want to talk with me or another team member a little more after we complete this meeting if this session does not seem to help."[6, 15]

Table 6.1 suggests possible interpretations for cognitive or affective reactions to stimuli or questions during a group crisis support session.

SUMMARY

This chapter covered several factors that are important for crisis team members. First, it addressed "active factors" in crisis support for groups. Five key active factors were identified: 1) the theoretical framework, 2) member characteristics, 3) leadership characteristics, 4) small group processes, and 5) group structure.

The issues of *structure, process, and content* relate to the factors that help the crisis team manage the group during group crisis intervention sessions. The most important factor is the power of the group, itself, to contribute to the support and healing of the members of the group.

The therapeutic factors identified by the world's leading expert on groups, Irvin Yalom, were described in detail. The three most important therapeutic factors in groups, as demonstrated by research are: 1) learning about oneself from group members, 2) catharsis, and 3) group cohesiveness.

The last group factor discussed in this chapter is the *domains* of human experience. The two domains described in this chapter are the *cognitive domain* and the *affective domain*. Cognitive domain has to do with the intellect; the affective domain deals with the emotions. Knowing which domain the group members are in during various stages of a group process is similar to having a map to guide the crisis team.

All of the major factors are interwoven during a group crisis support session. Obviously that can make a group intervention a rather complex interaction. Research, however, indicates several advantages to group intervention and points out directions for team members to follow to keep group crisis support manageable.

In the next chapter, large group processes will be described and differentiated from one another. Specific instructions for conducting large group interventions for primary groups will be presented. Subsequent chapters will cover large group interventions for secondary groups and interventions for heterogeneous groups. Interventions for small groups will be covered in later chapters.

Table 6.1.
Possible interpretations of group member reactions to questions.

Type of Stimulus/question	Response	Possible interpretation
None	Cognitive	Person wants to discuss event
None	Affective	Person wants to discuss emotions
None	Cognitive/ Affective	Person wants to tell their story and discuss their emotions
Cognitive	Cognitive	Person answers a question and shows willingness to engage in the discussion.
Cognitive	Cognitive / Affective	Person is willing to discuss most aspects of the situation.
Cognitive	Affective	Person wants to express distress or may have misunderstood the question. Emotions are coming to the surface
Affective	Cognitive	Person wants to avoid distress or may have misunderstood the question.
Affective	Affective	Person agrees to express distress. Engaged in process.
Affective	Affective / Cognitive	Person wants to discuss emotions and tell more of their story as well.

REFERENCES - Chapter 6

1. Solomon, Z., Shklar, R., Mikulincer, M. (2005). Frontline Treatment of Combat Stress Reaction: A 20-Year Longitudinal Evaluation Study. *American Journal of Psychiatry*, 162: 2309-2314.

2. Kyrouz, E. M., Humphreys, K. Loomis, C. (2002). A review of research on the effectiveness of self-help mutual aid groups. In B. J. White and E. J. Madara (Eds.). *Self-Help Group Sourcebook: Your Guide to Community and Online Support Groups*. Cedar Knolls, NJ: American Self-Help Clearinghouse / Saint Clares Health Services.

3. Davies, D.R., Burlingame, G.M, & Layne, C.M. (2006). Integrating small-Group Process Principles into Trauma-Focused Group Psychotherapy: What Should a Group Trauma Therapist Know? In L. A. Schein, H. I. Spitz, G. M. Burlingame and P. R. Muskin (Eds). *PsychologicalEffects of Catastrophic Disasters: Group Approaches to Treatment*. New York: The Haworth Press, 385-423.

4. Ettin, M. F. (1992). *Foundations and applications of group psychotherapy: A sphere of influence*. Needham Heights, MA: Allyn and Bacon, p.243.

5. Yalom, I. D. and Leszcz, M. (2005). *The Theory and Practice of Group Psychotherapy, 5th edition*. New York: Basic Books.

6. Dyregrov, A. (2003). *Psychological Debriefing: A leader's guide for* small group crisis intervention. Ellicott City, MD: Chevron Publishing Corporation.

7. Burlingame, G. M., MacKenzie, K. R., & Strauss, B. (2004). *Evidence based group treatment: matching models with disorder and patients*. Washington, DC: American Psychological Association.

8. Ulman, K. H. (2004). Group interventions for treatment of trauma in adults. In B. J. Buchele & H. I. Spitz (Eds.), *Group interventions for treatment of psychological trauma*. New York: American Group Psychotherapy Association.

9. Roberts, A. & Everly, G. S., Jr. (2006). A Merta-Analysis of 36 Crisis Intervention Studies. *Brief Treatment and Crisis Intervention*,6 (1), 10-21.

10. Schein, L. A., Spitz, H. I., Burlingame, G.M., Muskin, P. R. &Vargo, S. (Eds.) (2006). *Psychological Effects of Catastrophic Disasters: Group Approaches to Treatment*. New York: Haworth Press.

11. Burlingame, G.M., Mackenzie, K.R. & Strauss, B. (2003). Small group treatment: Evidence for Effectiveness and mechanisms of change. In M. Lambert, A.E. Bergin & S.L. Garfield (Eds.) *Handbook of Psychotherapy and behavior change, 5th edition*. New York: John Wiley and Sons, 647-696.

12. VandenBos, G., Editor in Chief. (2007). *APA Dictionary of Psychology*.Washington, DC: American Psychological Association.

13. Dies, R. R. (1994). Therapist variable in group psychotherapy research. In A. Fuhriman & G. M. Burlingame (Eds.), *Handbook of group psychotherapy: An empirical and clinical synthesis*. New York: Wiley, 114-154.

14. Foy, D.W., Glynn, S.M., Schnurr, P. P., Jankowski, M.K., Wattenberg, M. S., Weiss, D. S., Marmar, C. R. & Gusman, F. D. (2000). Group Therapy. In E. Foa, T. Keane & M. Friedman EDS.) *Effective* treatments for PTSD: Practice guidelines from the International *Society for Traumatic Stress Studies*. New York: Guilford Press, pp. 155-175, 336-338.

15. Mitchell, J.T. & Everly, G.S., Jr., (2001). *Critical Incident Stress* Debrief-

ing: An operations manual for CISD, Defusing and other *group crisis in-tervention services, Third Edition.* Ellicott City, MD: Chevron.

16. Olmstead, M.S. Hare, A. P. (1978). *The Small Group, 2nd edition.* New York: Random House.

17. Stockton, R., Rohde, R. I. & Haughey, J. (1992). The effects of structured group exercises on cohesion, engagement, avoidance and conflict. *Small Group Research, 23,* 155-168.

18. Burlingame, G. M., Fuhriman, A. & Johnson, J. E. (2002). Cohesion in group psychotherapy. In J. Norcross (Ed.), *Psychotherapy relationships that work.* New York: Oxford University Press, 71-88.

19. Bales, R. F. (1970). Interaction Process Analysis. In T. M. Mills & S. Rosenberg (Eds.) *Readings on the sociology of small groups.* Englewood Cliffs, NJ: Prentice Hall.

20. Bednar, R. L., Melnick, J., & Kaul, T.J. (1974). Risk, responsibility, and structure: A conceptual framework for initiating group counseling and psychotherapy. *Journal of Counseling Psychology, 21,* 31-37.

21. Egan, G. (1976). *Interpersonal Living: A skills / contract approach to Human-relations training in groups.* Monterey, CA: Brooks/ Cole Publishing Company.

22. Stockton, R. & Moran, D.K. (1982). Review and perspective of critical dimensions in therapeutic small group research. In G. M. Gazda (Ed.), *Basic approaches to group psychotherapy.* Springfiled, IL: Thomas.

23. Kaul , T. J. & Bednar, R. L. (1994). Pre-training and structure: Parallel lines yet to meet. In A. Fuhriman and G. M. Burlingame (Eds.) Handbook of group psychotherapy: An empirical and clinical *synthesis.* New York: Wiley, p. 161.

24. Janoff-Bulman, R. (1992). *Shattered assumptions: Toward a new psychology of trauma.* New York: Free Press.

25. Everly, G. S, Jr., Phillips, S. B., Kane, D. & Feldman, D. (2006). Introduction to and overview of Group Psychological First Aid. *Brief Treatment and Crisis Intervention, 6,* 130-136.

26. Fuhriman, A. & Burlingame, G. M. (1990). Consistency of matter: A comparative analysis of individual 4 and group process variables. *The Counseling Psychologist, 18,* 7-63.

27. Block, S., & Crouch, E. (1985). *Therapeutic factors in group psychotherapy.* London: Oxford University Press.

28. Layne, C. M., Saltzman, W. R., Steinberg, A. S. & Pynoos, R. S. (2003). *Trauma/ grief-focused group psychotherapy for adolescents.* Los Angeles, CA: national Center for Child Traumatic Stress.

Chapter 7

The Principles of Crisis Support for Large Groups

"I am a firm believer in the people. If given the truth, they can be depended upon to meet any national crises. The great point is to bring them the real facts."
~ Abraham Lincoln - *16th president of US (1809 - 1865)*

INTRODUCTION

Throughout history, charismatic leaders have stimulated large groups to take action and achieve great deeds. Stirring, large group, factual or informational presentations not only provide information and directions, but they enhance supportive relationships with peers, friends, and family members. They can inspire resistance to distress, along with the resiliency to "spring back" when stressed, and the ability to recover quickly.[1,2,3] Just two examples from the countless number of large group inspirations will be presented here.

At the famous battle of Marathon in 490 BC, Miltiades, the Athenian military leader, had to convince his 7,200 hundred troops that they could defeat a superior 20,000 man Persian force. They did exactly that and saved Greece from Persian occupation. Athenian losses were 192, but the Persians losses were in excess of 6,500 personnel. [4(pp.19-22)]

Historians point out how Winston Churchill, through his words, encouraged an entire nation to stand together against massive destruction, enormous loss of life, and a gripping fear of overpowering enemy forces with technology well beyond Britain's. On June 18, 1940, for example, he said, "The battle of Britain is about to begin…. Let us therefore brace ourselves to our duties, and so bear ourselves that, if the British Empire and its Commonwealth last for a thousand years, men will still say, 'This was their finest hour.'" [4 (p.245)] Churchill's speeches galvanized the British nation to successfully resist, despite overwhelming odds. And, with assistance from allied nations, Britain experienced a remarkable rebound and a recovery from the horrific traumas inflicted upon it.

Today, almost more than ever before, there is a need to work with large groups during times of crisis. Terrorism and warfare, natural and technological disasters, accidents, violent crimes, and mass migrations require more large-group crisis interventions than at almost any previous time in history. Some large groups are somewhat homogeneous (similar) in nature, such as large groups of fire fighters or law enforcement officers. Other large groups are heterogeneous (dissimilar) in nature. They may have experienced a traumatic event by being in the same space at the same time, but they really do not know each other and they do not have a relationship with each other. Travelers on an airplane would fall into the heterogeneous category. Each type of large group, homogeneous or heterogeneous, requires a different application of group intervention strategies and tactics. The same tactics cannot be used with both types of groups.

This short chapter will guide you through the principles and applications of crisis intervention for large groups. The material in this chapter is directly linked to concepts discussed in Chapters 4, 5, and 6. Familiarity with those chapters is, therefore, highly recommended.

ROOTS of LARGE GROUP INTERVENTIONS

Large group interventions did not recently show up as a result of traumatic events. There is a long history of the use of group didactic processes that can be traced back to at least the 1930s. Some clinicians organized lectures, homework, and even examinations for their client groups.[5] By the 1940s, some clinicians were organizing large group meetings in which they delivered lengthy lectures on the nervous system and its relationship to the group members' symptoms and disorders.[6]

One of the most prolific proponents of peer-run, psycho-educational programs was Abraham Low who founded Recovery, Incorporated in 1937. The primary function of this self-help group is to provide support to recovering psychiatric patients. Many of the Recovery, Incorporated groups are active today and are viewed as adjuncts to mental health treatment.[7, 8]

There are many other examples of small and large self-help groups that are functioning in a wide range of specialty areas, ranging from trauma intervention to bereavement and from medical problems to single parenting.[9, 10]

PRINCIPLES: CRISIS SUPPORT for LARGE GROUPS

A presenter of crisis intervention services for large groups does not have to be a powerful, inspiring speaker, as suggested in the historical examples in the introduction. What is necessary, instead, is knowledge of the principles of large group crisis intervention and the ability to distinguish between the requirements for large groups and those for small groups. Crisis response teams will have a much greater chance of providing successful support services if they keep the key principles in mind. There are numerous principles of group process that apply to large group interventions. Space and time does not permit a full presentation of every known group process principle. A summary of the key principles, however, is presented below. Read through these items and become very familiar with these group principles.

- The more *homogeneous* a group is, the more interactive it can be. The reverse is true as well. That is, the more heterogeneous a group is, the less interactive it can be.

- "In general...homogeneous groups jell more quickly, become more cohesive, offer more immediate support to group members...have less conflict, and provide more rapid relief of symptoms." [10] (p.272)

- Even in large group interventions, the aim should be to have groups as homogeneous as possible.

- Large groups are typically larger than 25.

- There is no ideal size, however, that is suggested for large groups. Much depends on the purpose of the group, the nature of the group and the level of organization which exists within the group. To some degree, the size limitations may depend on the complexity and intensity of the material to be presented to the group. If the object of a group meeting is to provide information alone, and is therefore predominantly didactic, the group size can actually be quite large, even in the hundreds.

- Educational or supportive group processes for homogeneous, non-clinical groups, such as fire fighters, police officers, emergency medical or military personnel who were exposed to a traumatic event, are **not** psychotherapy groups and they are not substitutes for psychotherapy. [9, 10]

- "Group size is inversely proportional to interaction." [10(p. 293)] The larger the group, the less interaction is likely to occur. Irvin Yalom, for example, found that in psychotherapy groups, when the number of members of a group increased, group interaction decreased. When the number in a group grew beyond a certain level, the interactions deceased substantially. [10]

- Defusing and the Critical Incident Stress Debriefing (CISD) should never be used with large groups or with heterogeneous groups. (See the later chapters on defusing and CISD.) [9]

- The longer the duration of the group session (within reason), the greater is the potential for interaction in the group. The most common form of interaction in a large group intervention is a question and answer period.

- In non-clinical (groups for purposes other than psychological treatment) educational or support groups (firefighters, police, etc.) group structure and control of the group processes can maintain greater group interaction with larger groups than would be seen in a psychotherapy group process. Again, large group interventions are not psychotherapy groups and comparisons between the two different types of groups are difficult to make and should be avoided.

- The more *homogeneous* a group, the greater the degree of affective domain (emotional) material it can manage.

- The greater the level of *heterogeneity*, the less affective domain material the group can manage.

- Primary groups are better able to tolerate and manage affective material than secondary groups. A random group is the least capable of managing affective material.

- If primary groups are too large (40 to 100 or more people) it is better to shift the focus to *cognitive material only*.

- If circumstances allow, subgroups of an extremely large primary group might be formed. Homogeneous subgroups, although still large, might allow more affective material to be managed in the group.

- Secondary groups usually cope better with cognitive material and little or no effort should be made to offer much beyond information and directions.

- Random or chance "groups" should *only* receive *cognitive* material.

- Question and answer periods are considered cognitive and should not be interpreted as affective. If a question brings in too much emotion for a group to handle, it is best to say something such as, "What you are saying is very important and you have some important questions regarding this subject. Let's meet after this session and we can discuss your concerns and see if we can answer your questions."

- A large group session can be used to as an early opportunity to assess the participants and determine which of the group members might need additional support or a referral for psychotherapy.

- Any individual who is acutely distressed before the large group intervention begins should be screened out and seen individually for crisis support and possibly a referral for further professional assessment.

- Information in a large group should always be *accurate, current, and timely.*

- Large groups should be clearly advised that the group process they are about to experience is *neither psychotherapy nor a substitute for psychotherapy.*

- A single group meeting may be helpful only if there are other support services combined into a comprehensive, integrated, systematic, and multi-component program of support.

- "The most successful leaders...were those whose style was moderate in amount of stimulation and in expression of executive function and high in caring and meaning attribution" [10] (p. 537)

HOMOGENEOUS vs. HETEROGENEOUS

The differences between homogenous (similar) and heterogeneous (dissimilar) groups is a central theme in group work, from the assessment stage through to the delivery of group crisis support and the appropriate follow-up services. Knowledge of the type of crisis-oriented group (large or small) must be matched with the nature of the group (homogeneous or heterogeneous). That match is essential for the success of any group intervention. The homogeneity or heterogeneity of a group is one of the most important factors in selecting the type of group crisis support. Considerable attention should be directed by a crisis response team toward deciding whether a group is homogeneous or heterogeneous.

Deciding whether a group is homogeneous or heterogeneous is actually a little more complicated than it first appears, because there are degrees of homogeneity or heterogeneity. At times, there may be an overlap between these terms; a group may be homogeneous in one regard, but heterogeneous in another. For example, if four men OR four women are gathered together, being male or female may make them homogeneous on the issue of gender. They can be, however, heterogeneous on almost every other consideration. If the four men or the four women are all police officers, they are now homogeneous on two issues within their separate groups (gender and profession). If all the males and all the females are blended together into one group, the eight police officers are now homogeneous on only one issue – being a police officer. The homogeneity of group by gender disappears when the male and female groups are combined. But, if the police officers come from four different states they are heterogeneous on many other issues, remaining homogeneous only on the issue of profession.

What we aim at in all group interventions are groups that are as evenly matched and as homogeneous as possible, so that that they can be thought of as if they were one unit. If all eight police officers are from the same jurisdiction, belong to the same squad, have the same responsibilities, the same leadership and training, and have worked together for six years, then they are truly a homogeneous group. When we are dealing with a larger group, greater degrees of heterogeneity will likely be found in the group.

The greater the number of items that can be checked on the list below, the greater the degree of homogeneity. Remember, we are dealing with large group interventions in this chapter, but, if we were focused on small group interventions, a very high level of homogeneity would be required. Small group interventions will be covered in subsequent chapters.[5, 6, 10-12]

Characteristics of members of homogeneous, PRIMARY groups

( ) Know each other

( ) Support each others' efforts

( ) Have friendship and respect for one another

( ) Have care and concern for each other

( ) Have frequent contact with one another

( ) Share the same philosophy of life

( ) Think in a similar manner

( ) Share the same goals and objectives

( ) Come from the same unit within an organization

( ) Have the same responsibilities

( ) Have similar backgrounds

( ) Have the same training

( ) Were in the same academy class

( ) Have the same leadership in the group

( ) Have a history of work together

( ) Work in the same jurisdictional area

( ) Are frequently on duty together

( ) Wear the same uniform

( ) Have had roughly the same exposure to a traumatic event

( ) See themselves as one unit

( ) Like to be together in a group

( ) Socialize together during off-duty time

The reverse of many of the above items indicates a heterogeneous group.

Characteristics of members of large, SECONDARY groups:

Armies, schools, businesses, church groups, neighborhoods and communities are homogeneous only in the broadest sense of the word. In actuality they do not share in many of the features previously described above which make a group truly homogeneous. Be careful not to assume homogeneity of group unless the members of the group are united on many of the features that would make them a primary group.

Characteristics of Members of HETEROGENEOUS groups

( ) Do not know each other

( ) May have only an acquaintance relationship, if any

( ) Are not considered friends

( ) Do not come from the same group, workplace, class, church, club, organization, agency, or community

( ) Do not have the same job

( ) Do not have the same training

( ) Do not share the same background

( ) Are not thought of as a single entity other than being part of a collection of people in the same place

( ) Are gathered together mostly by chance

( ) May only share in one or two issues such as a common interest in music or sports

( ) Have very little in common

TYPES of LARGE GROUP INTERVENTIONS

There are two main types of large group interventions. The first is *demobilization*; it is reserved for emergency operations personnel and military personnel, following their work at a major incident, such as a disaster.

The second type of large group intervention is a **Crisis Management Briefing**; it is much more frequently applied than the demobilization. It tolerates heterogeneity reasonably well. It is also a versatile group intervention process that has many applications.

Each of these will be discussed in detail in subsequent chapters.

IMPORTANT!

Group interventions, both large and small, should NOT be applied unless carefully timed. The critical incident should be finished or, at least, beyond its acute phases. The fundamental safety and security needs of the group must also be addressed before any group crisis intervention procedure is initiated.

SUMMARY

After briefly describing the roots of large group didactic interventions, this chapter presented 24 important principles of large group intervention. Many of the principles will also have applicability to small group interventions, so providers of all types of group services would be wise to keep them in mind.

The importance of homogeneity of group was then detailed. It cannot be overemphasized. Even in large groups, where crisis teams utilize a didactic approach, as much homogeneity of group should be present as possible. Finally, timing and the circumstances of group intervention were highlighted.

The next chapter will address the first of the two main interventions for large groups – **demobilization**.

REFERENCES - Chapter 7

1. Kaul, R. E. & Welzant, V. (2005). Disaster Mental Health: A discussion of Best Practices as Applied After the Pentagon Attack. In A. Roberts (Ed.) *Crisis Intervention Handbook: Assessment, Treatment and Research, 3rd Edition.* New York: Oxford University Press, 200-220.
2. Cowen, E. L., Wyman, P. A., & Work, W. C. (1996). Resilience in highly stressed urban children: Concepts and findings. *Bulletin of the New York Academy of Medicine,* 73, 267-284.
3. Mc Farlane, A. C., & Yehuda, R. (1996). Resilience, vulnerability and the course of posttraumatic reactions. In B. A. van der Kolk, A. C. McFarlane and L. Weisaeth (Eds.) *Traumatic stress: the effects of overwhelming experience of mind, body and society.* New York: Guilford pp. 155-181) .

4. Black, J. (Ed.). (2005). *The Seventy Great Battles in History.* New York: Thames & Hudson.

5. Marsh, L. (1935). Group Therapy and the Psychiatric Clinic. *Journal of Nervous and Mental Diseases*, 82, 381-390.

6. Jones, M. (1944). Group treatment with Particular Reference to Group Projection Methods. *American Journal of Psychiatry*, 101, 292-299.

7. Low, A. (1950). *Mental Health Through Will Training.* Boston, MA: Christopher Publishing House.

8. Murray, P. (1996). Recovery, Inc. as an adjunct to treatment in an Era of Managed Care. *Psychiatric Services*, 47 (1996), 1378-1381.

9. Mitchell, J.T. & Everly, G.S., Jr., (2001). *Critical Incident Stress* Debriefing: An operations manual for CISD, Defusing and other *group crisis intervention   services, Third Edition.* Ellicott City, MD: Chevron Publishing Corporation.

10. Yalom, I. D. and Leszcz, M. (2005). *The Theory and Practice of Group Psychotherapy, 5th edition.* New York: Basic Books.

11. Napier, R. W. & Gershenfeld, M. K. (1973). *Groups: Theory and Experience.* Boston: Houghton Mifflin Company.

12. Sharp, E. P. et al., Juvenile Division of the County Court (1962). *A primer of Short-term group counseling.* Philadelphia, PA:Youth Study Center.

Chapter 8

Crisis Intervention for Large Groups: Demobilization or "Post Operations Stress Information and Support"

"Of all the beliefs of the men and women in these pages, not the least important is faith in the power of personal connection to steer people through disaster."
~ John Rousmaniere *(sailor, maritime author, clergyman)*

"It is, after all, the human voice that stamps the mark of human consciousness upon the character of a gale" (Mirror of the Sea)
~ Joseph Conrad *(sailor, novelist)*

INTRODUCTION

The quotes for the header of this chapter deserve further comment. Both men were sailors who survived terrible storms at sea. Both men were significantly and permanently changed after their experiences. Rousmaniere notes, "in the chaos of any storm (whether at sea or on land), the norm at first seems to be alienation, not human contact." He then cites Joseph Conrad's experience of being alone on a night watch aboard a ship. He can hear the muffled voices of the men below decks. Conrad is surprised by finding comfort in the mere voice of a shipmate he actually dislikes. Rousmaniere quotes Conrad, *"It is, after all, the human voice that stamps the mark of human consciousness upon the character of a gale" (Mirror of the Sea).*[1]

Rousmaniere's remarks have application to all kinds of disaster. Experience indicates that people do tend to initially cut themselves off from others in the shock and chaos of the immediate aftermath of a disaster. For most people involved in a disaster, withdrawal, unless it is excessive, may not present any major problems. Withdrawal and isolation among military and emergency operations personnel may be more problematic. Since military and emergency personnel still have a job to do and may be reassigned or recalled to emergency duties with little warning, it is very important that they be guided back to group cohesion and the ability to perform as a unit as quickly as possible. There are psychological first aid tools that offer the best potential to achieve those goals.

Many a technical expert has said that choosing the right tool for the job is crucial for success, especially timely success. This chapter will discuss one of the large group crisis intervention tools – *demobilization*, which might more accurately be called *Post Operations Stress Information and Support* (POSIS). Whatever they are called, staff support services in the immediate aftermath of a disaster or other large scale operation are extremely important. Supportive services help fatigued personnel recognize that they are appreciated and valued by command personnel. The demobilization process enhances the recovery of unit cohesion and unit performance, which is a key element in maintaining a healthy work force.

Written and verbal feedback from thousands of operations personnel in many disasters suggests that the demobilization process is well received and appreciated. Demobilization is viewed as brief, to the point, and immediately helpful to operations staff. Crisis response teams are encouraged to carefully develop and present organized and well-managed demobilizations or "Post Operations Stress Information and Support" services.

DEMOBILIZATION

The word **demobilization** means a release from service. *Within a Critical Incident Stress Management (CISM) Program, it implies that a specially trained crisis response team member provides a limited amount of practical information to a relatively large group of operations personnel who have just completed their first shift at a disaster.* The information may help the members of the large group to let go of or "free up" some of the stress and tension that has built up during an intense, large scale operation like a disaster. Within the CISM field, **a demobilization is a large group informational meeting**. A demobilization service is essentially a brief rest period or a pause that occurs between the intensity of a major event and a reassignment to other less intense duties or a dismissal to home or to a rest facility. It gives tired military and emergency personnel a brief chance to receive instructions on ways to unwind after a difficult, distressing, or threatening mission. The demobilization is a simple informational process and can easily be delivered by a single person trained in CISM. Information is one of the very best stress reduction methods available.

IMPORTANT:

The word *demobilization*, in military thinking, refers to taking units, entire battalions, or even armies out of an operation, action, or service. When a unit is demobilized, it secures and packs its equipment and returns to its home base. The use of the word *demobilization*, as a large group crisis intervention tool, was borrowed from the military. It may produce confusion if used within military environments. It is therefore suggested that alternate wording be chosen for this large group crisis support process when used by military personnel. Within the military this large group process could be called a "rapid operational stress information session" or "a post operations stress information and support" service.

DEMOBILIZATION DETAILS

➤*Name of the Crisis Intervention tool*:

Demobilization or Post Operations Stress Information and Support (POSIS)

➤*Definition*

A **demobilization** is a brief, large group, informational, crisis-focused presentation for operations personnel immediately after their first work shift in a disaster or other major event.

➤*History*

The first demobilization services were conducted for fire and rescue personnel involved in the 1986 Cerritos, California, Aero Mexico air crash disaster. Then fire Captains Mel Hokanson and Wayne Ibers provided brief informational sessions for emergency personnel immediately after they completed their first work shift at the disaster site. Not long after, the demobilization process was utilized at the Amtrak train disaster in Chase, Maryland, in January, 1987.[2, 3] The process has been used on numerous disasters since then.

➤*Group size*

Demobilizations are typically comprised of 10 to 50 individuals, but may be much larger. Theoretically, the group size is unlimited since the purpose of the demobilization is simply to provide information. However, groups of more than 100 may become unwieldy and views of the speaker or of the audience, from the speaker's point of view, may be obscured. The guiding principles should be to do what needs to be done even if the group size is unusually large, but try to maintain reasonably-sized groups whenever possible. Sometimes, exceptionally large groups of emergency or military personnel may be subdivided into smaller groups and handled separately from one another.

➤ Timing of application

The demobilization is applied as personnel finish their first work shift before they go home or to other non disaster assignments.

➤ Can the demobilization be repeated?

NO! The demobilization should be used **only one time** with any group. The information would be repetitious and tedious if the demobilization is repeated for the same people. If groups need daily informational sessions on a multi-day incident, the Crisis Management Briefing (see Chapter 9) becomes the best tool for that purpose.

➤ Length of time

Thirty minutes; 10 minutes providing information and 20 minutes for rest and food.

➤ Location

Any convenient indoor environment can be utilized as long as it is near, **but not at**, the scene of the disaster. Sometimes, circumstances may force a crisis team to use a tent or even an outdoor meeting area. This is not ideal, but other options may be quite limited.

➤ Primary purposes:

- Information and guidance on managing distress
- Brief rest between the intensity of a major event and a return to normal duties
- Nourishment - food and fluids

➤ Key features:

- Brief (maximum 10 minute) presentation of information
- Rest, food, and fluids (typically no longer than 20 minutes)
- Directions or instructions from supervisors or commanders regarding return to alternate duties beyond the disaster or a release to home or a rest facility

➤ Target populations

The demobilization has been designed for only one use – the provision of stress management information for **emergency operations or military personnel immediately after their first exposure to disaster work** or to some other large scale highly stressful event. It is **not** to be used with the general public.

➤ Requirements

- Two large rooms (one for the informational presentations; the other for food and rest). It is helpful if several possible demobilization centers are designated before a disaster actually occurs. An appropriate facility, large enough to accommodate many emergency personnel at one time, is difficult to locate during a disaster situation.
- An adequate supply of tables and chairs for the food room and for the information area. Furniture should be movable. The facility should be appropriately air conditioned or heated. There should be sufficient light in which to work.
- An adequate supply of food and fluids for the personnel.
- Resources to restock food and fluids as they are consumed.
- One crisis team member who assumes the role of demobilization center manager and makes sure all aspects of the service run smoothly. The manager should also run the check-in desk, where disaster work crews report when they arrive at the demobilization center. The manager assigns them to one of many small circles of chairs where the information session will be provided by a crisis response team member.
- Six to eight CISM-trained team members who take turns and provide the informational component of the demobilization.
- Food staff to keep the food and fluids restocked.

- Sufficient parking to accommodate numerous emergency vehicles.

- Several police officers or other personnel who keep the media and other unauthorized people out of the area.

- A communications link to the command post to enable warnings about crew arrivals at the demobilization center. Communications with the command post allows for contact in the event of an unforeseen problem or questions that arise at the demobilization center.[4]

➤ Utilization rate

The use of the demobilization is quite rare simply because extremely stressful events, such as disasters, are typically very infrequent events. It may be used a little more frequently in the military.

➤ Goals and Objectives

- Practical information and directions for stress management
- Mitigation of the impact of a traumatic event
- Reduction of stress symptoms
- Rest and nourishment
- Rumor control
- Preliminary assessment
- Forewarning of potential problem area
- A transition from extreme action to normal duties
- Establishment of positive outcome expectancies in the group members
- Development of preliminary links for additional resources if they are necessary [5-8]

➤ Providers

The demobilization is provided by a peer support person or by a chaplain or mental health professional who has been trained in Critical Incident Stress Management. Crisis team members who served in the actual operation should **not** be presenters in a demobilization session. More likely than not, a person involved in the actual disaster operations will be emotionally "contaminated" by his or her exposure to the event and will not be able to provide adequate support to others.

➤ Organization

Successful demobilization services are no accident. They are carefully planned, hopefully in advance of a disaster, and skillfully managed. They will not work without command and administrative approval and endorsement. A demobilization service must work in concert, never in competition, with command and administration. Crisis team members should be trained and prepared before the disaster strikes. General written plans for a demobilization service can be enormously helpful in the midst of the chaos of a disaster. Handout materials should be printed and stockpiled. Here are a few other suggestions.

- Develop agreements with jurisdictions likely to respond on a mutual aid or disaster callout. Their personnel can then receive the same support services.

- An outline for the 10-minute presentation can be developed in advance and kept with the handout material.

- Preparatory drills are advisable.

- Have written agreements with potential sites before a disaster occurs. Also make sure that an easily accessible file, with current phone numbers and emergency contacts for the demobilization sites, is available.

- Educate all of the personnel in the emergency services agencies regarding the demobilization and its purposes and benefits before they ever have to attend a real one.

- It is helpful to brief the media in advance so that they do not interrupt the demobilization when it is in progress. Let them know that a demobilization is simply a method to rest work crews and provide them with useful information to manage the stress of disaster work.[4, 7]

➤ The process

Once a location for the demobilization has been selected, opened, and organized, command is notified that crews being released from the disaster site should be sent to the demobilization center for information, rest, and up-to-date direction from their command officers since they will not be returning to the disaster site until at least 6 to 10 hours have passed.[7] Units arriving at the demobilization center directly from the disaster site should

- be checked-in as a unit,
- kept in normal functional or work groups,

- be assigned a critical incident stress team member to provide the work group with **information on stress management** (limited to a **10-minute** period)

- be sent to the food room for **rest and nourishment for 20 minutes,**

- be informed that Critical Incident Stress Debriefings will be provided in the near future,

- be given a handout of pertinent stress management material,

- be thanked for their hard work in the disaster operation.

- be given instructions by a supervisor or command office regarding time off or reassignment to other duties.

►Specific topics addressed in a demobilization

The 10-minute stress management presentation should cover the following items:

- The crisis team member should introduce him or herself

- A brief description of the demobilization as an informational and rest program only.

- A statement that some people may already have stress symptoms, others may experience them later, and some will not have them at all.

- Assurances that, in any case, the symptoms are typically normal, healthy reactions to a highly stressful event.

- A review of some common stress symptoms.

- Presentation of several stress management "survival" suggestions to help the personnel through the next few days.

- The suggestions for managing the stress reactions include advice on eating properly, resting, avoiding alcohol consumption and the use of non prescription drugs, having positive contacts with family and friends, dealing with the media, and other helpful hints.

- Caution the group that they should seek additional support and guidance if the symptoms they are encountering become extreme or prolonged.

- Announce that Critical Incident Stress Debriefings will be arranged as soon as they are appropriate and when the group members are ready for them.

- Ask the group members if anyone has any questions or comments (It is rare to find members of a demobilization group who wish to speak when they are tired and still very close to the incident.)

- The crisis team member then summarizes the demobilization information.

- Handout material is distributed.

- Participants are thanked and directed toward the food room.[1-10]

►Complications

The organization of the demobilization is crucial to its success. Having a large enough facility with two large rooms, food, fluids, sufficient staff, washroom facilities, and communications can be especially challenging during a disaster. The demobilization center also needs chairs and tables, handout materials, and communications to coordinate with commanders. Finally, trained and skilled crisis team members are needed to deliver the information in the demobilization session. Below is a list of some of the more common problems encountered in a demobilization process for the operations personnel who are leaving a disaster site after their first work-shift. Most of the problems will be "people problems," rather than problems within the demobilization process itself. The majority of these problems, however, can be easily overcome by forethought and planning.

- Supervisors, commanders, and administrators who are not familiar with either the demobilization process or its benefits will sometimes resist or ignore the demobilization.

- Inadequate communications between command personnel and sometimes between commanders and the crisis response team.

- One problem that can arise when there is poor communications or misunderstanding of the demobilization is a premature release or reassignment of operations personnel before they can be given the support of the demobilization. Make sure all command personnel are notified of the demobilization process before personnel are released from on-scene duties in a disaster or other large scale incident. If a circumstance should occur in which personnel are released before the Post Operations Stress Information and Support (demobilization) services can be provided, there is one other option. Although less efficient than the large group demobilization, it is possible to partially substitute for the process by calling each operations person at home or in their stations to check on their welfare and give them some information.

- Another problem that will be generated by inadequate communications between the command post and the crisis response team is an overloading of the demobilization center by a too rapid or a simultaneous release of many different types of groups from the scene to the demobilization center, without a warning to the crisis team members. The other side of this communication problem is the failure on the part of command to advise and direct the groups that have completed their Post Operations Stress Information and Support session and are ready to go home or be reassigned to non-disaster duties. This will cause operations personnel, who should be moved out of the demobilization center, to "stack-up" and thus cause a backlog of operations personnel in the demobilization center. The groups that have completed the demobilization need to be released by a command representative; arrangements for transportation to their stations, home, or other assignments must be in place as soon as they complete the support session.

- An event may be of such overwhelming magnitude that demobilization is considered a low priority. This usually occurs when managers become short-sighted and think in immediate time frames instead viewing the long range negative effects of fatigued and unsupported personnel.

- There may be delays in notifying the critical incident stress management team that their services are required in the disaster. This problem can be solved by building in a system of automatic call-outs when certain things happen within an organization.

- There may be delays in opening the demobilization center. Designating sites in advance of a disaster and maintaining an accurate emergency contact list can do much to alleviate this problem.

- A demobilization center that is too far from a disaster, inconveniently situated, or too difficult to find will cause considerable frustration among the operations personnel. Plan in advance and select several potential sites within a jurisdiction, so that the closest and most convenient demobilization center can be chosen when a disaster occurs.

- Inadequate supplies of food and fluids. Again, pre-disaster arrangements can go far to eliminate this potential problem.

- An insufficient number of team members or having numerous CISM team members who are involved in fire suppression, search, rescue, field treatment, and recovery operations during the disaster. The best solution to this problem is to have mutual aid arrangements made in advance that facilitate the call-up of nearby crisis teams, able to fill in the crisis intervention services for local crisis team members who are directly engaged in the operations.

- The crisis team members providing the demobilization service must be very careful not to add problems to the Post Operations Stress Information and Support service by trying to do too much "helping." The demobilization is simple and easy. It should not be complicated by attempting to engage the personnel in in-depth one-on-one crisis support. Demobilization should only provide rest, information, and food before the personnel are released.

- No attempt should be made to provide a defusing or a Critical Incident Stress Debriefing (CISD). In disaster conditions, the defusing is replaced by the demobilization process. Do not provide both interventions to the same group. Furthermore, it is far too early for the CISD. Disaster work crews will need some time to wind down from their disaster work before they are ready to discuss their experience in a CISD. The demobilization session is clearly the wrong time, the wrong place, and the wrong set of circumstances for any small group services.

- Another potential problem occurs when the demobilization is overused. It is designed to be provided only one time, after the very first exposure to disaster. Using it on subsequent work shifts at the same disaster site is an overuse of this crisis intervention tool and will cause personnel to feel anger because the material is redundant. The scene has become more organized and the chaos of the first few hours of the disaster is substantially reduced. The demobilization is no longer needed, nor is it helpful when the circumstances are more organized than on the first exposure.

- Extreme exhaustion among operations personnel can be a major problem in demobilization. Exposure to the event may have drained their energy so much that they are incapable of absorbing the information in the demobilization. If severe fatigue is determined to be present in operations personnel, informational remarks can be shortened to only a few important comments. In some cases, it might be necessary to skip the informational phase of the demobilization altogether. Use common sense and good judgment in such cases. Keep in mind that the most important issue is to briefly rest and nourish the crews and then get them home or to new, non-disaster duties as soon as possible.

- Highly resistant personnel can present challenges for crisis teams. It would be best to carefully educate all emergency operations personnel long before a disaster occurs. But, if the disaster occurs before such education could be provided, then the crisis team member providing the information in the demobilization should acknowledge that some in the group might have a misperception of what the demobilization is. Assure the group members that they do not have to speak at all and that the crisis team will present only a few minutes of potentially useful information before the group is given some food and fluids. Keep the demobilization process simple and short and do not question the participants about their reactions to the event. All the demobilization should do is **"RIFR"** or *rest, inform, feed, and release* the group after its first exposure to the large scale operation.[1-10]

➤*Military adaptations*

The old adage, "Under extraordinary circumstances, ordinary rules of engagement no longer apply" fits well for crisis support services when many thousands of personnel are involved in an operation such as a major military mission. The most intense crisis support services, such as the small group defusing and CISD, must be reserved only for those units of operations personnel who experienced the most horrible aspects of a traumatic event. Those services may only be applied when the timing and the conditions are appropriate.

The immediate aftermath of a military mission does not offer the appropriate conditions for the use of those small group interventions. However, some support is necessary, so adaptations of what is used in the emergency services immediately after a traumatic exposure have to be made.

It was previously noted that the term **demobilization,** in itself, may be confusing when used in the context of military operations. The first change, therefore, is to call it something different. The recommended label is **Post Operations Stress Information and Support (POSIS)** service.

The Post Operations Stress Information and Support service can be utilized in the relatively immediate aftermath of a military operation, but a sensible approach has to be employed. There is a substantial amount of activity as military units complete their mission, gather, check, and clean their equipment, and maintain either a standby position or return to their assigned bases. The timing for the **POSIS** service must often be altered. Support services are difficult to provide if people are moving around and preparing for transport. It is also essential that personnel be out of danger when any support services are rendered. Immediate crisis intervention may be delayed for several days, and sometimes longer, to allow conditions to settle down. The primary rule for support services in regard to military units is that they should not interfere with the important duties of the personnel in the unit. A support service is not really supportive if it causes disruption and distress to the personnel in operational units.

The support process itself may need to be altered. It must be adapted to the needs of military personnel.

►Contraindications

There are circumstances for which the demobilization would be the wrong choice of supportive intervention. It is designed to provide information and rest to large groups of operations personnel immediately after their first exposure to the chaos of a disaster. Since disasters are rare occurrences for most local level emergency services organizations, demobilization-type support services are also rare.

Demobilizations or Post Operations Stress Information and Support services are **NOT** to be used in small scale, routine events, and **NEVER** as a substitute for small group support processes. Demobilization services are

- Not for routine emergency operations
- Not for small scale events such as minor fires and routine traffic accidents
- Never a substitute for defusing for small groups
- Never a substitute for Critical Incident Stress Debriefing for small groups of operations personnel
- Never used for line of duty death situations
- Never used for suicide of a colleague situations
- Not used on individuals, especially primary victims
- Not used except in large scale events such as disasters

►Follow-up

The reason for setting up a demobilization process, in the first place, is that large groups of operations personnel have experienced a disaster or other large scale event. In themselves, disaster situations are complex and intense. They generate widespread emotional reactions which typically need some attention in the weeks and sometimes months following the event. Follow-up after a demobilization or Post Operations Stress Information and Support service is vital. The information provided is helpful to personnel, but it is usually not enough for completion of the recovery process. There are many other things that may help to facilitate the recovery process. Here are some important follow-up services that should be part of a comprehensive, integrated, systematic, and multi-component crisis support program.

- Work site visits
- Phone calls to check on the welfare of the personnel
- Family support services
- Critical Incident Stress Debriefing
- Individual interventions
- Consultations with administration and supervisors
- Follow-up meetings
- Post incident educational programs
- Assistance in the documentation of lessons learned from the traumatic experience
- Referrals for those needing more than what crisis support can achieve[1-10]

SUMMARY

This chapter discussed one of several crisis intervention tools for groups. In this case it was the large group crisis intervention service called the *demobilization*. It was noted, early in the chapter, that the term *demobilization* has a very different meaning for military personnel and it was suggested that an alternate, and probably more accurate, term be used. It is suggested that "Post Operations Stress Information and Support" service be substituted for demobilization wherever the term demobilization causes confusion. The term Post Operations Stress Information and Support (POSIS) service certainly provides more information about the nature of this particular crisis intervention tool.

The next sections of the chapter provided complete descriptions of the intervention and specific, detailed guidelines to effectively deliver the service to emergency operations and military personnel who have been released from their first exposure to the chaos of a disaster or other major, large scale event. The reader was cautioned about the appropriate use of the support service and warned to avoid the process if certain conditions exist.

The demobilization or Post Operations Stress Information and Support service is a limited crisis intervention tool with substantial restrictions on its application. Some alterations must be kept in mind when working with military personnel. Whether they are working with emergency or military personnel, providers of the service should be properly trained. They should not deviate substantially from the specific guidelines presented in this chapter.

The next chapter will provide detailed coverage of the most commonly used and extremely versatile large group crisis intervention tool, known as the *Crisis Management Briefing*.

REFERENCES - Chapter 8

1. Rousmaniere, J. (2004) *After the Storm: True Stories of Disaster and Recovery at Sea.* New York: International Marine / Mc Graw-Hill, xii, 268.
2. Mitchell, J. T. (1991). Demobilizations. *Life Net,The Newsletter of the International Critical Incident Stress Foundation,* vol.2, (1).
3. Hokanson, M. (1997) *Evaluation of the Effectiveness of the Critical* Incident Stress Management Program for the Los Angeles County *Fire Department.* Los Angeles, CA: LACoFD.
4. Mitchell, J.T. & Everly, George, S., Jr. (2001). *Critical Incident Stress* Debriefing: An Operations Manual for CISD, Defusing and Other *Group Crisis Intervention Services (3ʳᵈ Edition).* Ellicott City, MD: Chevron Publishing.
5. Everly, G. S., Jr., Lating, J. M., & Mitchell, J. T. (2005). Innovations in Group Crisis Intervention. In A. R. Roberts (Ed.), *Crisis Intervention Handbook: Assessment, Treatment and Research (3ʳᵈ Ed.)* New York: Oxford University Press, 221-245.
6. Eaton, Y. M. (2005) The Comprehensive Crisis Intervention Model of Safe Harbor Behavioral Health Crisis Services. In A. R. Roberts (Ed.), *Crisis Intervention Handbook: Assessment, Treatment and Research (3ʳᵈ Ed.)* New York: Oxford University Press, 619-631.
7. Mitchell, J. T. & Everly, G. S. (2006). Critical Incident Stress Management in Terrorist Events and Disasters. *In L. A. Schein, H. I. Spitz, Burlingame, G. M., Muskin, P. R. (Eds.)* New York: The Haworth Press, 425-480.
8. Mitchell, J.T. & Everly, G. S. (2003). *Critical Incident Stress Management (CISM): Group Crisis Intervention (3ʳᵈ edition revised).* Ellicott City, MD: International Critical Incident Stress Foundation.
9. Mitchell, J. T. (2006). *Critical Incident Stress Management (CISM): Group Crisis Intervention (4ᵗʰ Edition).* Ellicott City, MD: International Critical Incident Stress Foundation.
10. Everly, G. S., Jr. (2000). Crisis Management Briefings (CMB): Large group crisis intervention in response to terrorism, disasters, and violence. *International Journal of Emergency Mental Health,*2 (1), 53-57.

Chapter 9

Large Group Applications of the Crisis Management Briefing

As a general rule the most successful man in life is the man who has the best information."
~ Benjamin Disraeli - *British politician (1804 - 1881)*

INTRODUCTION

Information is the operative word in all large group interventions. This is particularly so in the case of the *Crisis Management Briefing* process that is the focus of this chapter. People in distress frequently need information to lower their anxiety, assist them in making decisions, and guide their actions in controlling and resolving the situation. There are very few psychological first aid tools that are as versatile or as effective in delivering important information to large groups of people as the *Crisis Management Briefing*. Over the last decade, this tool has been used not only with its original intended audience of emergency and military operations personnel, but also with schools, businesses, industries, churches, organizations, and communities. Feedback from participants in these sessions indicates that this large group information session is appreciated and valued. Its practical approach makes it very helpful. Terrorism and other large scale traumatic events are likely to keep this beneficial tool in use for the foreseeable future.

CRISIS MANAGEMENT BRIEFING

In general terms, a Crisis Management Briefing (CMB) is a semi-structured gathering of people who are impacted by the same disturbing event and who are in urgent need of information to assist them with their efforts to manage the situation or their reactions to it.

CRISIS MANAGEMENT BRIEFING DETAILS
➤ Definition

The **Crisis Management Briefing (CMB)** is an intervention technique designed for use with large groups. It is a meeting with a specific purpose of providing practical, hopefully stress-diminishing, information to a large group of people who have already experienced, or who are about to experience, a distressing event.

➤ History

Applications, in one form or another, of large group interventions, such as the CMB, can be traced back to the foundations of group crisis intervention.[1-6] Large group, informational processes, in addition to the demobilization-approach described in the previous chapter, were certainly an integral part of Critical Incident Stress Management programs throughout the 1980s and 1990s. The CMB was not actually named, however, until 1999.[7-12]

➤ Group Size

Depending on circumstances and the type of group to be addressed, group size may be quite variable. It is not unusual to have up to 300 people in a CMB. In cases of biological, nuclear, incendiary, chemical, and explosive threats, the CMB may be used to address mass audiences in the thousands by means of television, radio, and internet services.

➤ Timing of Application

The CMB sessions are so versatile that they can be used in a wide range of circumstances. A CMB may be provided just *before* a large group is exposed to a distressing experience. For example: a community had been safely evacuated in advance of approaching flood waters. Much destruction had occurred in their town before the water receded. The only scenes the citizens had been able to see were taken from a news helicopter flying over the town. Finally, the authorities were ready to allow the townspeople back into town to see the damage to their properties. To lessen the emotional shock of suddenly going into a destroyed town to see their damaged properties for the first time since the flood, a CMB was presented by the crisis team.

CMBs may be presented periodically *during* an ongoing event. Informative updates can be provided to people impacted by the distressing situation.

Sometimes CMBs can be provided every eight to twelve hours, if circumstances are rapidly changing. Usually, they are given once a day if changes in the situation are occurring slowly.

CMBs can also be provided immediately *after* a traumatic event ends. They have been used, often within an hour or so of the ending of a threatening or frightening event, in businesses, industries, and schools to provide useful information and guidelines for recovery from the traumatic incident.[13]

►Can the Crisis Management Briefing be repeated?

Yes, definitely! The CMB may be used as often as necessary as the conditions in the situation change. Of course, it is strongly recommended that new content be added each time the CMB is used during a particular event. There is a need for some repetition of information from previous CMBs, but if new information is not added, those who are personally impacted by the event will become frustrated and angry. Most likely they will react negatively toward the crisis team as the team's credibility deteriorates.

►Length of Time

Most CMBs are completed within 30 to 45 minutes. Occasionally, up to 75 minutes may be required if there are several officials who have information to contribute, in addition to the crisis team's presentation on stress management. The length of time also depends on the number and types of questions asked during the CMB.

►Location

The preferred location is a large indoor meeting facility that has sufficient seating to accommodate the number of people who are attending. The facility should be air conditioned or heated appropriately and it should be well lighted. Restroom facilities are essential. It is helpful if one or two smaller meeting rooms are available in case a few people need individual crisis intervention after the CMB.

Although indoor facilities are most desirable because they offer a greater degree of privacy, there have been occasions in which CMBs have had to be presented in the outdoors or under a large tent. The crisis team must be flexible enough to work under less than ideal circumstances.

➤ *Primary Purposes*

To provide information to reduce emotional distress in large groups of people who are dealing with a disturbing, threatening, or traumatizing event.

➤ *Key Features*

- A facility large enough to accommodate those who wish to attend is required.
- The "Town Hall" style meeting is introduced and led by a member of the crisis response team.
- One or more appropriate officials (school, health, police, fire, emergency management, business leader, etc.) are introduced by the crisis team member; they then make a presentation of facts about the situation.
- The crisis response team member presents information on stress management and guidelines for managing the emotional aspects of the situation.
- The attendees may ask question to clarify points and gain additional information. The crisis team member will moderate the question period.
- The crisis team member summarizes and concludes the session.

➤ *Target Populations*

Large groups. Homogeneous groups are preferred, but the CMB can easily be adapted for work with diverse, heterogeneous groups.

➤ *Requirements*

- A large meeting space
- An official representative of the organization, agency, company, school, or church, who can provide factual information on the situation to the group.
- A knowledgeable and skillful crisis team member to facilitate all aspects of the CMB and present information on stress and crisis management.
- Accurate, current, and timely information.

➤ *Utilization Rate*

The use of the CMB is quite frequent since information is extremely important in reducing distress. As experience with the CMB increases, crisis teams are using the technique more frequently than ever before.

➤ Goals and Objectives

- Provide information
- Control rumors
- Reduce the sense of chaos
- Provide coping resources
- Facilitate follow-up care
- Engender increased cohesion and morale
- Assess further needs of the group
- Restore personnel to adaptive functions

➤ Providers

The CMB uses a team approach. One or two crisis team members partner with officials from the impacted organization, company, church, school, or agency. The officials present the factual information; the crisis team members present the information on stress and the guidelines for managing the emotional aspects of the situation.

➤ Organization

Decisions to apply the CMB should be based on the crisis team's assessment of both the situation and the reactions of those involved. Once the decision is made, the crisis team member assigned to manage the CMB must meet with the authorized official or officials who will be delivering the factual information about the situation. A plan of presentation, which includes details of the information to be given to the large group, must be agreed upon. Then determination must be made as to whether one meeting session will be sufficient or whether several nearly identical meetings are necessary to handle the size of the group. It is also important for the team to know the level of similarity or diversity that exists in the group. Once the content of the meeting is determined, specific meeting times and other details should be addressed.

➤ The CMB Process

Assemble the participants. Keep in mind that at least a minimal degree of homogeneity (same neighborhood, same street, same organization, etc.) is preferred.

Officials from the appropriate organization(s) are introduced by the crisis team member; they present factual information, directions, and guidance on the incident. It is especially important that the officials use this opportunity to instruct people about the steps they should take to protect themselves and manage the situation. Sometimes a question and answer period regarding the incident occurs after the officials make their remarks.

A stress and crisis management presentation is made by the crisis team member. The distress of the participants should be acknowledged and validated. The emotional impacts of traumatic events are described and the signs and symptoms of distress may be discussed, including certain behaviors to be aware of which might indicate a potential problem. The emphasis in this phase is on normalizing the stress reactions of the group members.

The crisis team member then provides many practical suggestions on stress management and how to deal with an emotional crisis. To start the closure stages of the CMB, the crisis team conducts a questions and answers period. Before concluding, the crisis team member makes sure that there are no additional pressing questions. The crisis team member then summarizes the meeting and offers any conclusions that are necessary. If additional meetings are warranted, the crisis team member may suggest the next meeting time and place.

►*Specific Topics Typically Addressed in a CMB*

- Facts regarding the situation.
- Approximate time before situation is resolved.
- The current and future potential dangers related to the situation.
- The measures that emergency services personnel are currently taking.
- The amount of damage that has already occurred.
- The number and types of casualties sustained thus far.
- Descriptions and locations of appropriate resources for the community members.
- Information that dispels rumors.
- Guidance on safety, security, shelter, food, and other essentials.
- Descriptions of the typical emotional reactions to a traumatic event.
- Normalization of those reactions.
- Lists of potential signals of distress that some people might encounter.

- Any information that mitigate the emotional reactions to the traumatic event.

- Any information that can lower anxiety.

- Any information that guides people to appropriate behaviors, such as checking in on elderly people in the neighborhood until the situation is resolved.

- Practical steps to take in handling personal distress and the distress experienced by children, the elderly, and any other special populations.

- Suggestions on diet, exercise, rest, sleep, decision making, and problem solving.

- Any other information that appears to be needed should be presented before the crisis team members summarizes and concludes the CMB.

► Complications

There are several potential complications that might influence a CMB. Here are some that present a challenge to crisis team members:

Media representatives are present in the group. The CMB is not a press conference and should not be treated as such. It is better if the media are not present. Keeping the media out may not always be possible. When they show up at a CMB, they should be advised that interviews and any information that would normally be addressed in a press conference will be handled after the CMB. Let the media representative know that the CMB is really for the benefit of the members of the community that has been affected by the traumatic event and all question should relate to the needs of the community members. It is preferable that the media withhold their questions until officials can meet with them separately.

Very angry group. On occasion, a group may be intensely angry when the people conducting the CMB arrive at the meeting. Politics, personal issues, cultural issues, misperceptions of the actions of officials, and a host of other conditions may be behind this high level of anger. When the anger is so extreme, the CMB team has several options. They might present information only and avoid a question and answer period. Or, they might meet with community leaders privately to see if the leaders can help calm the crowd. Or, if the situation is simply too hostile to given a fair hearing, the CMB team might opt to postpone or even cancel the CMB meeting.

Worsening conditions arise during the presentation of the CMB. Every once in a while, a situation can deteriorate while a CMB is in progress.

A message arrives to the CMB team that weather conditions are deteriorating or that a person who was injured and was being treated at the hospital has now died. Any number of negative conditions can arise during the CMB. It is best to give the bad news to the audience as early as possible in the CMB. It may need to be incorporated into the presentation. If the group is in immediate danger (for example, the wind has shifted and a poisonous cloud is now heading toward the meeting) the people need to be directed to safety and the meeting stopped.

Authorized officials are too distraught to effectively deliver information. Sometimes authorized officials are too upset to be effective in the delivery of information. If no officials can be found to take their place in the CMB, the crisis team member may have to assume the role of the designated officials and provide the information himself, or draw upon the services of another crisis team member who can present the facts of the situation after consultation with appropriate officials from the organization or community. Under such circumstances it is helpful to have written notes from which the remarks are made.

➤ *Military Adaptations*

The CMB has been used in military situations, including combat. It is important that immediate dangerous situations be eliminated or well controlled before any attempt is made to provide the type of information that is usually presented in a CMB. It is also advisable that military operations personnel are given a period of "down time" before being brought together for the CMB. The down time can vary, but at least 45 minutes is desired. Personnel can use the time between the event and the presentation of the CMB to take care of personal needs, to clean and ready weapons and other equipment, and to unwind a little after the disturbing experience. The CMB should always be thought of as just one step in a series of supportive steps to assist operations personnel in staying healthy and functioning at maximal performance levels. Other crisis support services should always be available for implementation with military personnel when they are necessary.

➤ *Contraindications*

The CMB should **NOT** be used in the following conditions. A package of other group and individual crisis interventions are more suitable under such circumstances.

- *Suicide of a colleague*, when the crisis team is dealing with a small, homogeneous group. (Please see the chapters to follow on small group crisis support).

- *Line-of-duty death* (also known as death-in-service or workplace death), when the crisis team is assisting a small, homogeneous group. (See the chapters on small group crisis support.)

- *When gathering a group together intensifies risks*, such as when there is a considerable risk of a terrorist attack or when an epidemic is spreading. The use of radio, television, and the internet are obviously safer approaches.

➤ Small Group Adaptation of the CMB

Several small group interventions are thoroughly discussed in Chapters 10, 11, and 12. There is one alteration of the CMB that is applicable to small groups, however, and it is, therefore, worthy of a brief discussion here. A CMB may be used with a small, **heterogeneous** (mixed) group. That is, when there are 2 to 20 people who know little or nothing of each other and do not interact with each other, but who have experienced the same distressing event, they may be given a CMB. The format is the same, but the discussion is less formal and more conversational. The emphasis, of course, remains on the provision of practical information. Affective discussions are generally avoided. If an individual in the mixed group begins to discuss affective material, the crisis team group leader simply needs to say something on the order of, "What you are bringing up is extremely important, can you and I meet after this session and discuss it? I have some thoughts on that issue that may be helpful to you." Do not be abrupt in cutting off such discussions, but they need to be managed separately to keep the mixed group from hearing too much disturbing detail about the event or a specific individual's reaction to that event.

➤ Follow-up

Throughout this book the provision of a "package" or a program of crisis intervention tactics or techniques is emphasized. The Crisis Management Briefing (CMB) is no exception. Like virtually everything else in the crisis intervention field, it is not a stand-alone tactic. It must be used as a part of a broader intervention program. Follow-up to a CMB is required. Phone calls, work site visits, conversations with supervisors, individual contacts, and referrals are some of the many follow-up services that may be required. Crisis team members must be alert to the needs of the people they serve. They must be innovative and flexible in finding ways to continue to follow up until they are assured that the individual members of a mixed group, such as those encountered in a CMB, are well on their way to recovery and a resumption of normal life functions.

SUMMARY

This chapter concludes the discussion of informational meetings for large groups. It discussed one of the most useful tools in the crisis intervention "tool box" - the Crisis Management Briefing (CMB). This versatile tool has applications before a large, heterogeneous group is exposed to a distressing experience; it has applications while an event is ongoing; and it can be used immediately or with a brief delay after a traumatic situation ends.

The CMB requires planning, teamwork, and cooperation with the administration of a jurisdiction, an organization, an agency, a business, or a community. The crisis response team works together with representatives of whatever group is requesting support. The most informative and helpful program is developed for presentation to the group. The CMB is typically applied to heterogeneous groups (mixed groups who do not know each other or who have different functions).

CMBs have been provided in a wide range of traumatic experiences including murders, accidents and gas leaks. They have also been used in disasters and terrorist attacks. No doubt, they will be necessary for the foreseeable future.

The next chapter on *defusing* begins the discussion of small group crisis intervention processes. Small group support services are more interactive than large group interventions. They focus a little less on the cognitive aspects of a traumatic event and allow a homogeneous group to interact with each other and with a crisis team to work through a disruptive or traumatic event.

REFERENCES - Chapter 9

1. Marsh, L. (1935). Group Therapy and the Psychiatric Clinic. *Journal of Nervous and Mental Diseases*, 82, 381-390.

2. Jones, M. (1944). Group treatment with Particular Reference to Group Projection Methods. *American Journal of Psychiatry*, 101, 292-299.

3. Low, A. (1950). *Mental Health Through Will Training*. Boston, MA: Christopher Publishing House.

4. Murray, P. (1996). Recovery, Inc. as an adjunct to treatment in an Era of Managed Care. *Psychiatric Services*, 47 (1996), 1378-1381.

5. Mitchell, J.T. & Everly, G.S., Jr., (2001). *Critical Incident Stress* Debriefing: An operations manual for CISD, Defusing and other *group crisis intervention   services, Third Edition.* Ellicott City, MD: Chevron Publishing Corporation.

6. Yalom, I. D. & Leszcz, M. (2005). *The Theory and Practice of Group Psychotherapy, 5ᵗʰ edition.* New York: Basic Books.

7. Everly, G.S., Jr. & Mitchell, J.T. (1999). *Critical Incident Stress management (CISM): A new era and standard of care in crisis intervention.* Ellicott City, MD: Chevron Publishing Corporation.

8. Everly, G.S., Jr. (2000). Crisis Management Briefings (CMB): Large Group Crisis Intervention in Response to Terrorism, Disasters, and Violence. *International Journal of Emergency Mental Health,* 2 (1), 53-57.

9. Newman, E.C. (2000). Group crisis intervention in a school setting following an attempted suicide. *International Journal of Emergency Mental Health,* 2, 97-100.

10. Mitchell, J.T. & Everly, G.S. (2004). *Critical Incident Stress Management (CISM): Group Crisis Intervention, 3ʳᵈ Edition.* Ellicott City, MD: International Critical Incident Stress Foundation.

11. Castellano, C. (2003). Large Group Crisis Intervention for Law Enforcement in Response to the September 11 World Trade Center Mass Disaster. *International Critical Incident Stress Foundation,* 5(4), 211-215.

12. Mitchell, J.T. (2006). *Critical Incident Stress Management (CISM): Group Crisis Intervention, 4ᵗʰ Edition.* Ellicott City, MD: International Critical Incident Stress Foundation.

13. Gibson, M. (2006). *Order From Chaos: Responding to traumaticevents, revised 3ʳᵈ Edition.* Bristol, UK: The policy Press, University of Bristol.

Chapter 10

Crisis Support for Small Groups: Immediate Group Support with Defusing

"Never doubt that a small group of thoughtful, committed citizens can change the world. Indeed, it is the only thing that ever has."
~ Margaret Mead - *US anthropologist (1901 - 1978)*

IMPORTANT!
Small group crisis support processes are for **HOMOGENEOUS** groups only.

INTRODUCTION

In this Chapter we enter the realm of crisis support for small groups. In large groups, the emphasis was solely on the provision of helpful information. The emphasis on practical information does not disappear in small group crisis intervention. It remains a focus, but many features are added to the processes for small groups. For instance, there is more interaction between the support team and the group members. Group members may discuss some of their personal reactions. The group members support one another. The information given by the support team is more specific to the needs of that particular group.

In the CISM field, the first of the two main interventions for small groups is the *defusing*. As the name implies, this small group process is designed to neutralize a situation or remove the fuse from a distressing condition before it can become an "emotional bomb." A defusing can be a powerful crisis intervention tool if it is used in the very early stages of a crisis reaction. It lowers tension and "buys" us a little time to set up other support services.

IMPORTANT!
To be maximally effective, a defusing must be provided
within a few hours of the end of the event.

In Chapters 4, 5, and 6 substantial information on group principles, group dynamics, group transactions, and group leadership was presented. If readers are a little unsure of those important group issues, it would be advisable to read through those chapters before proceeding with small group interventions.

DEFUSING

A ***defusing*** *is a brief, small group crisis support service that is provided within hours of the exposure of a homogeneous group to a traumatic event.* It is a semi-structured discussion of the experience, led by a trained team of peer support personnel after the completion of the event.

A quick analysis of the previous paragraph indicates that there are several central concepts of defusing that should be highlighted. These defusing concepts are fundamental and are so important that a failure to understand them may result in a misapplication of the defusing process. So they are listed below:

- A defusing is brief.
- It is a process for small groups.
- A defusing occurs within hours of an event.
- A defusing is only provided when a group has been exposed to a traumatic event
- The group must be **homogeneous** (alike).
- A defusing has some structure, but it is **not** a very rigid discussion.
- A defusing is led by a trained peer support team.
- The critical event must have reached its conclusion before a defusing takes place.

DEFUSING DETAILS
➤ *Definition*

A **defusing** is an immediate, brief, group discussion of a traumatic event for a small, homogenous group.

➤History

The term *defusing* entered the CISM literature in 1983. It appeared in the very first article ever written on Critical Incident Stress Debriefing (CISD). At that time it was called "The Initial Defusing." It was described as a shortened type of CISD.[1] Shortly after the publication of that first article, the word *initial* was dropped and it does not appear in later publications.[2] The defusing has been consistently used since the mid 1980s. In most areas, crisis teams utilize the defusing a little more frequently than they use the CISD.

➤Group Size

The ideal size for an interactive, homogeneous group defusing process is two to twelve group members. Sometimes somewhat larger groups are acceptable if the group is, indeed, a homogeneous group.

➤Timing of Application

The defusing has been specifically developed for immediate application, timed as closely as possible, within reason, to the conclusion of a traumatic event. The small group defusing process has the greatest potential to stabilize the reactions of a group to a bad situation when it is used within eight hours of a traumatic event. That first eight hours is a period of vulnerability for distressed and stunned personnel. They are most open to further disruption during this time. They are also most open to external support during the same vulnerability period. Support services are generally accepted and appreciated during this period. Carefully applied early support develops rapport with the distressed personnel and enhances the potential success of crisis contacts in the next few days.[3, 4, 5]

➤Can the Defusing be Repeated?

<u>No</u>, not with the same group on the same incident. The defusing was designed for a single use with a specific homogeneous group. If there is an unusually large homogeneous group, it may be divided into several smaller groups. Only one defusing is provided for each of the subgroups on a particular incident.

There is no problem in doing a defusing with the same group on some future event. A new event is a new trauma for the group and therefore a new defusing is appropriate.

➤ *Length of Time*

A defusing is short. Most range between 20 and 45 minutes. The average defusing lasts approximately 30 minutes. Concern should rise if a defusing goes beyond an hour. Either the event is enormous and overpowering or the crisis team is demonstrating poor understanding of the defusing process and possibly inadequate leadership during the defusing.[6]

➤ *Location*

A defusing can be held in almost any location that is quiet, uninterrupted, and protected from the media. The preference is an indoor setting, such as a conference room or a classroom. Defusings have also been provided in the engine room of a fire station and in the living room of someone's home. They may be held outdoors as long as the area is private, the temperatures are comfortable, and there is a place for all of the participants and the crisis team members to sit.

➤ *Primary Purposes*

- To mitigate the impact of a traumatic event on an emergency services, a military unit or some other small homogeneous group. .

- To facilitate unit cohesion and a return to normal unit functions.

- To provide an opportunity for a preliminary assessment of which members of a group are doing well and which ones might benefit from an individual contact with a crisis team member.[7]

IMPORTANT!

The defusing is NOT any form of psychotherapy, counseling, or medical or physical treatment, nor is it a substitute for any of those processes.

➤ *Key Features*:

- A defusing is led by a trained team of peer support personnel, such as firefighters, law enforcement personnel, military personnel, emergency medical services personnel, dispatchers, nurses, pilots, school crisis support personnel, or railroad engineers.

- There are three segments: a) *introduction* of the crisis team and presentation of the working rules of the group meeting, b) brief *exploration* of the event, and c) *information* to assist the personnel in managing traumatic stress and returning to normal functions.

- Immediate individual support to group members exhibiting signs of distress during the defusing meeting.

►Target Populations

A defusing is only used for **homogeneous groups** who have together encountered the same highly stressful event.

►Requirements

- An event of sufficient magnitude to distress an operations group.
- Homogeneity of group - this is the primary requirement. Homogeneity is absolutely required in small group interventions. If it is not present, the small group process should not be provided.
- A properly trained peer team.
- A private meeting place.
- Administrator or supervisor approval, since the meeting often takes place while personnel are on duty and on departmental property.
- Sufficient time to complete the process.

►Utilization Rate

The defusing is used, on average, between 1 and 3 times per month for the typical Critical Incident Stress Management team. Much of the utilization rate depends on the size of the population and the number and type of traumatic events that occur within a particular jurisdiction during an average month. A wide range of variation can be seen with the utilization rates of defusing. This occurs for many reasons, including the occurrence of events, the knowledge and skill of the CISM team, and whether or not members of a group issue calls for assistance with a particular tragic event.

►Goals and Objectives

- Mitigation of the impact of an event on a work crew or unit.
- Reduction in the signs and symptoms of distress.
- Facilitation of the recovery process

- Assessment of need for additional services.

- Assessment of individuals within the group who might benefit from additional support services.

➤ Providers

Only trained Critical Incident Stress Management team members should provide a defusing. Most often the team consists of two peer support personnel. Once in awhile, a CISM mental health professional or a chaplain is available and may work with the peer support personnel during the defusing.

➤ Organization

The call for the defusing may come from one of several sources. For example, if a traumatic situation occurs and a trained CISM team member is part of the operational unit in the field, he or she might alert the team to the need for response. In other situations, a supervisor or an officer calls for the team. Or perhaps a hospital nurse may note that a crew seems distressed and calls out the team.

In any case, once the team has been alerted to the occurrence of a traumatic event, the coordinator calls the person requesting assistance and obtains further details. If the situation warrants a defusing team, the team members are selected and given a briefing on the situation. They then proceed to the defusing location, meet briefly with supervisors or command staff, and confirm what is known of the case. The crisis team decides which among them is best suited to be the leader for the defusing group process. The responsibilities of each crisis team member are quickly reviewed and the brief planning session ends. The group is brought together and the defusing is conducted.

➤ The Defusing Process

- Choose a private location.

- Arrange the chairs around a conference table or in a small circle.

- Phase 1 – Introduce the team members, explain what the defusing is and why it is being conducted; give the guidelines that help the defusing to run smoothly.

- Phase 2 – Ask questions that open up the brief discussion. It is usually best to say something such as, "We have information from our team that may be helpful to you, but we can give you the best information if we know what you just went through. It would help our team to have a brief description of the situation."

- In phase 2, once the conversation starts, it is important for the crisis team members to ask several other questions that help to give a reasonably clear picture of the circumstances of the event. Avoid, however, efforts to dig too deeply. This phase represents only a broad overview of the situation.

- Throughout the defusing process, **please, absolutely avoid asking how people feel.** "Feeling" questions cause people a great deal of embarrassment and discomfort in a small group process. No one likes to discuss their feelings in front of their colleagues. Remember, this is not therapy in any form. It is simply a conversation about a traumatic event.

- When sufficient information and discussion has taken place, the questioning stops and the team moves the conversation toward the final phase. Longer pauses after each new question and less information being presented by the group participants with each new question suggest that the conversation is coming to a close.

- Phase 3 consists of a presentation of information that normalizes the reactions of the personnel and guides them in stress survival tactics and recovery processes.

- A defusing should affirm the value of the personnel and develop expectancies for the future.

- Finally, the defusing should end with a decision by the crisis team as to whether or not a full CISD is required or if other types of follow-up services need to be offered.

➤ Specific Topics Typically Addressed in a Defusing

A defusing process attempts to do as many of the following as possible.

- Calm emotions
- Reduce cognitive, emotional and physical distress
- Encourage group member discussion
- Clarify basic information about the situation
- Enhance group cohesion and mutual support for one another
- Allow a brief time for rest and some time to "gather one's thoughts"

- Inform group members about steps to take for stress management
- Assess the members of the group to determine who might need additional support and who will do fine without additional support
- Assess the need for a CISD or other support services
- Link participants to other resources if they should need them.

►Complications

Time is the greatest enemy in providing a defusing. The longer one waits, the less effect a defusing will have. One hour is a better time to provide the defusing than is two hours. Two hours is better than five hours. And five is better than eight. Once you are beyond the 8 to 12 hour range, you should conclude that too much time has elapsed; the team should therefore resort to individual contacts with each member of the impacted unit. Arrange a CISD several days later and do whatever can be done until the CISD takes place.

A second enemy in defusing is administrative ignorance of or interference with the crisis intervention program. This problem can be easily eliminated or better managed if pre-incident education and information programs, regarding the applications and benefits of the many support services of the CISM system, are provided within the organization.

Another complication occurs when the administration is backing the crisis support service and the personnel want it, but the mission is prolonged and personnel cannot be released to go to the defusing. In such cases, the crisis team should provide individual support until the situation clears and a defusing can be held.

One final complication occurs in circumstances in which the personnel are so physically and emotionally drained that they are unable to participate in the defusing process. It would be foolish to try to force a defusing under such circumstances. The crisis support team should simply assess the situation realistically, provide individual support where necessary, and set up a CISD for several days later after people have had a chance to rest and physically recover. [7,8]

►Military Adaptations

The defusing has already been used in military missions, including combat operations. The same complications are in effect for the military as mentioned in the previous section of this chapter. Additionally, combat stress control units may be too few and too spread out in a large scale operation, such as the war in Iraq, to be immediately effective in all cases of traumatic stress. Medics, platoon and other unit leaders should, therefore, be taught the key elements of "psychological self aid and buddy care," so that a defusing can be conducted at the unit level once a traumatizing mission draws to a close. Psychological support services, obviously, are secondary to unit safety and mission completion. But, once units are safe, it would be helpful to bring the small group together for a quick, supportive defusing session. Not all missions will need this support service. It should be reserved only for the missions that cause great disturbance for the unit members. If the circumstances of the operation are overwhelming and likely to leave long lasting psychological effect, unit commanders and medics should have available to them the services of a combat stress control unit. Keep in mind that the overall aim of a defusing is unit cohesion and the rebuilding of unit performance.

➤ Contraindications

The defusing is contraindicated in the following circumstances.

- **With individuals**. It is especially contraindicated with individuals who are primary victims of a traumatic event. That is, **the defusing process should never be used with individuals**, such as those who are victims of auto accident, sexual assault, burns, dog bites, miscarriages, difficult pregnancies, and physical injuries.

- **With heterogeneous groups**. If the group is a mixed group, defusing should not be used.

- **In disasters**. Instead, rely on demobilizations (Chapter 8) for operations personnel and the Crisis Management Briefing (Chapter 9) for community members.

- **In the case of Line of Duty Deaths**. The defusing is not a sufficient crisis intervention tool to manage the severe impact of a line of duty death. The five-phase adaptation of the Critical Incident Stress Debriefing (see the section on five-phase CISD in Chapter 11) should be used for homogeneous groups attempting to cope with a line of duty death.

➤ Follow-up

Follow-up services are always required when a defusing has been selected as the crisis intervention tool. Some people will need more follow up than others. In most groups, some group members are fine and need no additional services after a defusing. Follow-up should continue until the support team is confident that recovery is occurring or until a referral for either additional support services or further evaluation is made. Follow-up contacts typically number between one and five. The following "rule of thumb" may be helpful in deciding whether further follow-up or a referral is most appropriate.

Number of crisis intervention contacts	Decision Guidance
3-5 crisis contacts	3 to 5 contacts is the acceptable standard in crisis intervention
6-7 crisis contacts	referral may be necessary if the crisis reaction does not appear to be close to resolution
8 or more crisis contacts	referral for professional services is indicated

➤ Is the defusing process effective?

It should be noted that few people have specifically studied the defusing process. There are, however, two studies that are particularly applicable in this discussion. The first was performed by Yvonne Evans, when she was a graduate psychology student at Loyola College in Baltimore in the early 1990s. She developed an interesting, experimental research protocol in which she studied the immunoglobulin (antibody) levels in the saliva of fire and emergency medical personnel immediately after a traumatic exposure, but before they participated in a defusing provided by trained CISM team members. The personnel were assessed again immediately after the completion of the defusing. She also developed a comparison category of trauma-exposed emergency personnel who gave saliva samples after a traumatic exposure, but did not participate in the defusing. They were reassessed within a period of time in which immunoglobin levels were expected to return to normal levels after a traumatic experience. There were greater beneficial changes in the immunoglobin levels among the personnel who had participated in the defusing than in those who had not.

The experimental research design and the results are quite interesting, but the study was unfortunately never published because the number of participants was fewer than desired. This occurred for a number of reasons including the unpredictability of traumatic events, the immediate availability of a saliva sample collection kits, the availability of trained personnel to collect the samples, and the difficulties of cooling and transporting the saliva samples to a laboratory for evaluation within specific, limited time frames. Furthermore, there was considerable expense associated with the laboratory procedures.[9]

The second study specifically on the defusing process by J. De Gaglia in 2006 is a comparison between groups of Florida-based fire and rescue professionals who either participated in the small group defusing process, or who received no intervention and relied instead on the natural healing that occurs with the pasage of time. The defusing "...significantly lowered the composite negative affect score, whether compared to the preintervention score or the trauma-exposed group who were 3 days distant from the trauma but had received no intervention" (p. 308).[9] The fire and rescue professionals who participated in the defusing process stated that they were more likely to seek out future mental health serivces and future small group interventions. The author of the study, J. De Gaglia, states that the study results do not only indicate an immediate benefit of defusing for the participants, but that they were more than twice as likely to seek future support than those who did not receive the defusing.[10]

SUMMARY

In contrast to the relatively easy informational presentations for large groups explored in Chapters 8 and 9, processes for small groups, such as the defusing, require a great deal more interaction between the crisis intervention group leaders and the participants. Small group leaders must manage the sequence of the discussion and be alert to the subtle signs that individuals within the group are having a difficult time with the traumatic experience. In a defusing the crisis team needs to formulate their questions based on the discussion as it evolves since there are no preset questions.

Obviously, interventions for small groups, such as the defusing, present greater challenges to the provider and therefore require a greater degree of training. Training in group crisis intervention skills is provided around the world by instructors approved by the International Critical Incident Stress Foundation (ICISF). To find a training program in your area, contact ICISF on its website, www.icisf.org and review the calendar section.

The next chapter will cover the most difficult of the group crisis support services. It is the **Critical Incident Stress Debriefing (CISD).**

REFERENCES - Chapter 10

1. Mitchell, J.T. (1983) When disaster strikes ... The critical incident stress debriefing process. *Journal of Emergency Medical Services*, 13 (11), 49 – 52.

2. Mitchell, J. T. (1988). Development and functions of a critical incident stress debriefing team. *Journal of Emergency Medical Services*, 13(12), 43-46.

3. Crocq, L. (1999). *Les traumatisms Psychiques De Guerre.* Paris: Odile Jacob.

4. Campfield, K. & Hills, A. (2001). Effect of timing of Critical Incident Stress Debriefing (CISD) on posttraumatic symptoms. *Journal of Traumatic Stress*, 14, 327-340.

5. Caplan, G. (1964). *Principles of Preventive Psychiatry.* New York: Basic Books.

6. Mitchell, J.T. (2006). *Critical Incident Stress Management (CISM): Group Crisis Intervention, 4th Edition.* Ellicott City, MD: International Critical Incident Stress Foundation.

7. Mitchell, J.T. & Everly, Jr., G.S. (2006). Critical Incident Stress Management in Terrorist Events and Disasters. In L.A. Schein, H.I. Spitz, G. M. Burlingame, P.R. Muskin, S. Vargo (Eds.). *Psychological Effects of Catastrophic Disasters: Group Approaches to Treatment.* New York: The Haworth Press.

8. Mitchell, J.T. (2004). *Critical Incident Stress Management (CISM): Group Crisis Intervention, 3rd Edition.* Ellicott City, MD: International Critical Incident Stress Foundation.

9. Evans, Y (1997) Personal Communication.

10. De Gaglia, J. (2006). Effects of small group crisis intervention (Defusing) on negative affective and agreeableness to seeking mental health services. *Brief Treatment and Crisis Intervention*, 6, 308-315.

Chapter 11

Crisis Support for Small Groups: Critical Incident Stress Debriefing

"From this day forward until the end of the world...we in it shall be remembered...we band of brothers."
~ 'Henry V', William Shakespeare,
English dramatist & poet (1564 - 1616)

INTRODUCTION

Shakespeare's quotation above, selected as a banner for this chapter, introduces the most fundamental requirement for crisis support for small groups – homogeneity of group. The concept of a homogeneous group (like a band of brothers) is so essential that it is a "Sine Qua Non" of small group crisis support. Sine qua non is a Latin phrase and its literal translation is, "Without which... none." Without a homogeneous group, crisis support for a small group is unwarranted. Use individual crisis intervention techniques instead or a Crisis Management Briefing for heterogeneous groups. Small group, in the context of this book, typically implies a homogeneous group. As defined in Chapters four, five and six, a homogeneous group is one in which its individual members are so bonded together as to be thought of as if one. Together, the members of a small group must be a unit.

The focus of this chapter is the specific crisis support process for small groups known as the *Critical Incident Stress Debriefing* (CISD). Recent research indicates that CISDs generate consistently positive results if trained, skillful crisis team members, who adhere to the protocols, provide the intervention (see chapter 12).

THE TERM, "DEBRIEFING"

The generic term, *debriefing*, has so many different loosely defined or even ill defined meanings today that it is now the source of considerable confusion. Therefore, it should be clear from the start of this chapter that there are many different types of *debriefings* and that one type of *debriefing* is not equivalent to another type. The Central Intelligence Agency, for instance, uses the term *debriefing* as a mechanism to gather and organize useful information from its field agents who are returning after an assignment. The military uses the term to gather information about what went right and what went wrong with a mission in order to improve future operations. The military also uses a *debriefing* to determine enemy strength and weaknesses and to develop better strategic plans. In search and rescue services, a *debriefing* is the process that search planners use to gather information about the quality of a search to determine if more resources are necessary in a particular search sector or if those resources would be more useful elsewhere. Businesses and industries use *debriefings* to adjust their development, manufacturing, advertising, sales, and distribution of products. Most of these organizations are reasonably close to the basic definition of *debriefing* as it appears in dictionaries. That is, a *debriefing* is a process of questioning people to gather important information.

Unfortunately, in the psychosocial field, the term *debriefing* has frequently been diluted, distorted, misinterpreted and broadly applied to a wide range of processes ranging from individual conversations to the provision of group information within an educational setting. Some use *debriefing* to describe unspecified support services. Others use the term as a label for counseling services. Some mental health professionals even use the term *debriefing* when they refer to psychotherapy processes. A number of professionals erroneously confuse the generic term *debriefing* with the specific process of the *Critical Incident Stress Debriefing*. It is common to hear professionals from the same profession using the term *debriefing* in enormously different ways at the same conference. It is, therefore, extremely difficult to carry on rational conversations or professional discussions when the same term is defined and applied in so many different ways.

There is so much confusion generated by the psychosocial community's lack of discipline in both the definition of and the use of the word *debriefing* that some crisis support teams and even entire organizations are trying to find alternatives to the word. A cautious, thoughtful decision-making process is required before making any conclusions regarding name changes. Name changes, at this time in history, may be premature. Name changes are more complex then they appear at first glance. A name change can actually result in a greater degree of confusion in the field. It may be a more realistic solution to the problem to promote the elimination of the generic term *debriefing* altogether within the psychosocial field and a restriction of the term *Critical Incident Stress Debriefing* for use only when referring to the specific, seven-phase, crisis support process for small groups, which will be described later in this chapter.

IMPORTANT!
The term *debriefing* has too many meanings. Do NOT use the term in a psychosocial context. It is certainly NOT equivalent to *Critical Incident Stress Debriefing*.

TYPES of PSYCHOSOCIAL DEBRIEFING

The Critical Incident Stress Debriefing (CISD) is the most well-known and most widely practiced crisis intervention process for small groups in the world.[4] More than 1000 critical incident stress management teams in 28 nations around the world use the CISD process when they are working with small groups of distressed people. However, before moving onto a detailed discussion of the specific CISD process, please note that other crisis intervention models for groups exist. For example, S. L. A. Marshall developed one approach to group work in World War II and it ultimately influenced the development of the CISD process. Several other models appear to be offshoots of Marshall's model and the CISD model.

S. L. A. Marshall's *Historical Event Reconstruction Debriefing* model

Brigadier General Samuel Lyman Atwood (S. L. A.) Marshall was a military historian who interviewed soldiers, sailors, and marines during World War II and for some time after the war. He frequently interviewed military units together in a "historical group debriefing" soon after battle. His objective was to develop a comprehensive historical record of the main combat operations and significant battles of the war. He did a remarkable job. His published contributions generated many changes in military strategies and tactics. Today, military officers in many nations study Marshall's historical records, books, articles, and recommendations.

As Marshall interviewed individual soldiers, platoons, or specialty teams, he discovered that the majority of military personnel expressed relief and appreciation for the opportunity to discuss their combat experiences. Many stated that they felt that huge psychological burdens became less painful and that they experienced a "spiritual purge" when they spoke about the war. They also stated that the debriefing was a "morale building experience." [5 (p.215), 6, 7]

Since World War II, military psychologists and psychiatrists were well aware of Marshall's work and his conclusions. They formulated assessment and support programs for military personnel, which eventually evolved into modern Combat Stress Control Programs. Israeli military psychiatrists, in particular, used Marshall's interviewing techniques as the basis for their own combat stress control programs. There is, therefore, a great emphasis placed on the systematic, moment-by-moment experience of a soldier during an operation. The Israeli military forces experienced substantial reductions in disruptive stress reactions by using combat stress services based in part on Marshall's work.[8]

Marshall's work was a considerable influence when the Critical Incident Stress Management system and the specific CISD support tactic for small groups was developed in the mid 1970s.

Atle Dyregrov's *Process Debriefing* model

Atle Dyregrov, a psychotherapist and researcher in Bergen, Norway, is the first to protest that he did not develop a separate debriefing model, but that he simply emphasizes different elements of the existing CISD model and utilizes the group members to provide assistance to one another. Many refer to his approach to CISD as "Psychological Debriefing" and erroneously insist that it is a different model than CISD.

In any case, Dyregrov has contributed enormously to the world's understanding of and application of crisis intervention procedures for small groups. Crisis teams that provide CISDs to small groups would be wise to adopt many of his guiding principles for small group processes. If they did so, they would greatly enhance both their group management skills and the positive effects they have on small groups. Every person serving on a Critical Incident Stress Management team should read his book, *Psychological Debriefing: A leader's guide for small group crisis intervention.*[9]

NOVA's *Group Crisis Intervention* model

The National Organization of Victim's Assistance (NOVA) has developed a group-oriented, crisis intervention model. It actually goes by the label, "Group Crisis Intervention." In many ways, it is similar to the CISD; but there are some differences. Most importantly, its focus is to support the actual victims of a traumatic event. The CISD, on the other hand, concentrates on emergency services and military personnel as its first priority. The Nova model has less focus on personal thoughts and more emphasis on future expectations in the aftermath of a traumatic experience. There is also less emphasis on symptoms of distress and more emphasis on stress education. The NOVA model is one phase shorter than the CISD.[10]

ARC's *Multi-stressor Debriefing* model

The American Red Cross developed the Multi-Stressor Debriefing model for its staff members who had experienced a prolonged deployment. It is three phases shorter than a CISD and there is more emphasis on feelings and coping methods.[11]

J. Stokes' *Critical Event Debriefing* model

Colonel James Stokes developed the Critical Event Debriefing for the military. The CISD process influenced Stokes' model, as did Marshall's debriefing approach. It is one phase shorter than the CISD and emphasizes the chronological event. It combines cognitive and affective elements in the same phase. It also emphasizes information and education for soldiers.[12]

ICISF's *Critical Incident Stress Debriefing* model

Critical Incident Stress Debriefing (CISD) refers **only** to the specific, seven-step, support process for small homogeneous groups described in detail below.

CRITICAL INCIDENT STRESS DEBRIEFING DETAILS

From this point forward, in this chapter, we will discuss only the Critical Incident Stress Debriefing (CISD) model of small group crisis support.

➤*Name Of Crisis Intervention Tool*

Critical Incident Stress Debriefing (CISD) – NOT   simply "debriefing"

➤*Definition*

*A **Critical Incident Stress Debriefing (CISD)** is a structured, seven-phase, small meeting for a homogeneous group to discuss the group members' reactions to a mutually experienced traumatic event.* The discussion aims at reducing stress reactions and enhancing group cohesiveness and group performance.[13, 14]

➤*History*

The story of the CISD began in the early 1970s when I was a graduate psychology student at Loyola College in Baltimore. After a series of traumatic events as a firefighter and paramedic and after watching several colleagues prematurely leave emergency services, I combined my knowledge of emergency

Table 11.1

Similarities and Differences between the Main Types of Psychosocial Debriefings.

Critical Incident Stress Debriefing Mitchell	Process Debriefing Dyregrov	Group Crisis Intervention NOVA	Multi-Stressor Debriefing ARC	Critical Event Debriefing Stokes	Historical Event Reconstruction Debriefing Marshall / Shalev
Introduction	Introduction	Introduction	Event	Introduction	Introduction
Fact	Fact	Event	Feelings & Reaction	Chronological Reconstruction	Chronological Reconstruction
Thought	Thought	Aftermath	Coping	Cognitive, Affective Reactions	
Reaction	Sensory	Expectations of Future	Termination	Symptoms	
Symptom	Normalization	Education		Teaching	
Teaching	Closure	Conclusion		Wrap - up	
Re – entry	Follow-up Debriefing				

Table 11.1 was developed by Dr. George S. Everly, Jr. and is used with his permission.

services personnel with the knowledge I was gaining in the areas of psychology and crisis intervention. I researched every article and book I could find all the way back to the early 1900s when crisis theory began to evolve in Europe.

By 1974, I developed the general outline of what eventually became the present day CISD process for small group crisis intervention. At that time, I was also speaking about stress management at emergency services conferences. The question and answer periods in those presentations indicated to me that emergency personnel were in great need of information and support concerning the management of traumatic stress. Shortly after one of these presentations, a fire officer asked me to intervene with a group of emergency operations personnel who had handled a gruesome scene in which several young children had died. I quickly recruited a social worker, who was comfortable with group work, to help me. We responded to the agency's request for group crisis support. The year 1974, therefore, marks the first year in which a formal Critical Incident Stress Debriefing occurred. Although the traumatic event was extremely painful for the personnel involved, my colleague and I received much appreciation for our efforts with the group. The specific feedback from the group members about the CISD process, however, was invaluable beyond description. That terrible tragedy set the stage for the crisis support systems that have developed since that time.

Nine years later, the first peer-based and mental health professional guided Critical Incident Stress Management team sprang to life in Alexandria and Arlington Counties in Virginia. Two decades and a few years later there are more than 1,000 CISM teams serving their emergency personnel and their communities in 28 nations around the world. All of these crisis response teams use the Critical Incident Stress Debriefing process for small groups as part of a comprehensive, integrated, systematic, and multi-component approach to crisis intervention within their communities.

IMPORTANT!
Always use A Critical Incident Stress Debriefing within a program of other crisis support services.

➤ Group Size

The *ideal group* size is between 2 and 10 people. The *typical group* size is between 8 and 25 people. It is generally best to avoid groups larger than 25. If a group size becomes too large, the CISD process may be impaired.[13, 14]

➤ Timing of Application

The timing of a CISD is important. The *ideal time* for a CISD is 24 to 72 hours after the conclusion of the critical incident; it takes approximately 24 hours for people to become physically calmed and mentally ready for the CISD process.[15] A rule of thumb is: the stronger the impact of the event, the longer is the time-frame before the CISD loses its power. Psychological readiness on the part of the group is more important than the passage of time. We should aim at achieving the maximal positive effect by matching the availability of the CISD with the psychological readiness of the group.

Disasters present a highly unusual case in which CISD may be delayed for several weeks and sometimes longer. Several research projects and clinical experiences describe positive outcomes involving delayed CISD interventions for small groups.[16, 17]

➤ Can the Critical Incident Stress Debriefing be Repeated?

No, do not repeat the CISD. Apply it one time for each homogeneous group involved in a distressing event. It is fine to use it on the same group if a new event arises, but not on the same group concerning the same event. The CISD, however, is **not** a stand-alone intervention. Use the CISD in conjunction with other crisis support services. A CISD should always be part of a package of interventions, including family support, individual contacts, post-incident education, and follow-up services.

The CISD process is not a stand-alone intervention. At the very least, follow-up support is required for some people in every CISD.

➤ Length of Time

A CISD generally takes between one and three hours. The difference in time depends on two things: 1) the number of participants and 2) the intensity of the event. Larger groups and more intense situations usually extend the time beyond the average of one and a half hours.

➤ Location

Pick as comfortable a room as possible. The location should be large enough to accommodate the entire group as well as the crisis team members. Ideally speaking, the CISM team providing the CISD controls the lights and the air conditioning or heat. Seats should be comfortable. A single access door is preferable and the room should be private, not open to view by outsiders.

We can discuss the criteria for CISD locations at length, but often CISM team members have to contend with a broad range of facilities. Some are impressive and some are depressing. Team members have learned to adjust to whatever location is available for a CISD and make the best of it.

►Primary Purposes

The main purposes of a CISD are to moderate distress and enhance unit cohesion and unit performance in a homogeneous group that has encountered a disturbing and disruptive event.[13, 14]

►Key Features

A CISD has several key features. They are:

- A CISM team facilitates the CISD process. The team typically numbers between two and four people depending on the size of the group.

- The typical ratio is one team member for every five to seven participants in the small group. One team member is a mental health professional. The others are peer support personnel. Add a chaplain to the team if one is trained and available for the meeting.

- The CISD has a seven-phase structure.

- The CISD team respects the rights of individuals not to actively participate if they choose not to. Never force a person to speak.

- Everyone has a right to speak openly if he or she wishes to do so.

- The CISM team provides immediate follow-up after the CISD session ends.

- The team functions on a basis of interactive leadership. Although there is always one primary leader, any of the other team members may ask questions and provide feedback. With experienced teams, a peer may lead in one CISD and the mental health professional may lead in another.

- The telling of the story of the incident (fact phase) is actually a small portion of the CISD. The most emphasized phases of the CISD are the reactions phase and the teaching phase.

- Every team member contributes something to the teaching phase and each one makes a brief summary remark in the re-entry phase.

- Follow-up is always required when a CISD is complete. The follow-up begins immediately and is most often in the form of individual contacts.

➤ Target Populations

Homogeneous groups are the target of CISDs. The group should be a single entity or unit. Typically, schedule the CISD for law enforcement personnel from the same unit, companies of firefighters, military units, paramedic personnel, airline crews, train crews who work together regularly, a school class, or other small homogeneous groups such as, employees from the same company, or members of the same organization in the aftermath of a serious and disturbing event. All of the participants in the CISD should have experienced the same event, which, of course, is complete before the CISD is scheduled.

➤ Requirements

The requirements to conduct a CISD are:

- An adequately trained and experienced team.
- A homogeneous group.
- Unit exposure to the same seriously distressing event.
- The mission or the critical event concluded or well past the most acute stages.
- A private setting.
- Refreshments for a gathering of the participants when the CISD concludes.

   Do not provide a CISD if the group is not homogeneous.

➤ Utilization Rate

Utilization rates for the CISD can vary widely depending on a number of factors including:

- population density,
- geography, natural hazards, potential for disastrous events,
- frequency, type and duration of traumatic events,
- number of CISM team members,

- level of community violence,
- past experiences with traumatic events,
- community awareness of the team,
- organizational awareness and trust in the team,
- pre-incident education programs,
- effectiveness of past interventions.

Newly formed teams tend to have approximately one small group CISD call-out per month. As a team matures, it usually provides more education to its constituents between calls. It also provides more defusing services closer to the occurrence of the event. Finally, it increases the number of individual contacts. Once education, defusing support, and individual contacts increase, the number of CISDs tends to decline, sometimes by as much as 50%.

➤Goals and Objectives

A CISD has only three primary goals or objectives.

- Mitigation of impact of a stressful event on the personnel in a homogeneous group
- Facilitation of recovery processes in normal people who are experiencing normal stress reactions to a terribly abnormal event
- Identification of individuals within the group who might benefit from additional support or a referral to other resources

➤Providers

Only a team of appropriately trained professional and peer support personnel should lead a CISD. The training consists of eight to ten days of special courses. Two days consist of group training; two days composed of assisting individual in crisis; two days of suicide prevention, intervention and recovery training; two days of advanced group crisis training and two days of strategic crisis intervention training. Each team member must complete at least the two-day group crisis course before assisting in a CISD with other team members who have completed more training and who are more experienced.

➤Organization

Each team has at least one team coordinator. A dispatcher in the communications center typically receives a call for assistance after a critical incident. The dispatcher then gathers pertinent information from the caller and contacts the on-duty CISM team coordinator. The dispatcher describes the nature of the request to the team coordinator. The team coordinator then contacts the original caller and obtains further information. Once the coordinator confirms the need for a CISD or other crisis support services, the coordinator calls other team members and develops a response team and a strategic intervention plan. It is important to clarify all of the important details pertinent to the response, such as the date, time, location, and response team objectives. Briefing the response team members before deployment is essential to assure that the best support. The team leader assigns specific functions to team members according go their training and skill level. The team members work under the direction of the team leader to gather more information, assess individual members of the group, and set up the meeting room.

➤ The Seven-Phase CISD Process

Two factors are constantly interacting during a small group process like a CISD. First, there are the domains of human experience – cognitive and affective. A thorough discussion of the domains is in Chapter 6 of this book. The second factor is the seven-step structure of the CISD. CISM team members must be alert to the interactions of these two factors and skillfully guide the group through the seven phases while allowing the participants to express themselves in the cognitive or affective domains.

The seven phases of the CISD process are:

1. Introduction

Introduce the CISM team members and describe the CISD process. Then describe the guidelines for the CISD and encourage the group members to participate and discuss their experiences and reactions. It is important to motivate the group members to assist one another by discussing their views. Encouragement is important, but it should not be overdone. The participants in a CISD have an absolute right not to speak. Therefore, CISM team members must be careful not to exert pressure on the participants. Notify participants that their involvement in the discussion is voluntary. The team discusses any additional ground rules before beginning the CISD.

2. Fact

The title of this phase of a CISD may cause some readers to think that the CISM team is interested in many specific details about the event. This is not the case. Rather, detailed renditions about specific critical facts are **not** required and are discouraged. All the CISM team actually needs is a very brief thumbnail sketch of the event. A few sentences from the participants are usually sufficient. The fact phase merely gets the participants talking, but it is not the essence of the CISD. The question that is most often used in the fact phase goes something like this: "Please tell our team who you are; what your role was during the incident; and give us a very brief description of what happened from your point of view." In essence you are saying, "Give us a thumbnail sketch of the experience as you saw it. Lots of details are **not** needed. Just give us the big picture."

In most CISDs, in the fact phase, the leader goes around the room from left to right or right to left and gives everyone an opportunity to speak freely if they wish. The fact phase is a collection of descriptions of external circumstances and occurrences related to the distressing event. *The discussion remains in the* **cognitive domain***.*

3. Thought

The thought phase is a very important *transition phase from the cognitive domain* of the fact phase *toward the affective domain* in the reaction phase. The thought phase allows a gradual movement into the potentially uncomfortable realm of discussing emotionally laden content.

The thought phase is one in which the participants begin to take some "ownership" of their experience. When the question, "What was your first thought or your most prominent thought during or immediately after the incident?" is asked in a CISD, group members who describe their thoughts "own" some piece of the experience. Thoughts about an experience are internal and personal. *The thought phase has* **mostly cognitive domain** *features, but it "opens the door" to the affective domain.*

The team leader again guides the participants and systematically moves the discussion from one group member to another and allows each person to present their thoughts. If someone does not wish to speak, a simple shake of the head or wave-off of the question signals the facilitator to move onto the next person. This is the last phase in which the leader goes sequentially around the room in the CISD.

4. Reaction

The reaction phase is the heart of CISD. Frequently, it is also the longest segment. *It is an* **affective phase***.* That is, the reaction phase is a discussion of affective material. In the reaction phase the question is asked, "What is the very worst thing about this event for you personally?" Another way to ask the question is, "If you could go back to the incident and there was one thing that you wish you could magically erase with the outcome remaining about the same, what would be the one part you would most want to be erased?"

Just because a phase is labeled as an "affective phase" does not mean that the people in the group have to break down and cry. In fact, crying is rare in most CISDs. However, with or without tears, emotional expressions are perfectly fine. However, team members should be careful not to draw attention to the person who cries. Crying is quite normal and, in a CISD, it is usually short in duration; but the embarrassment of having a team member pay too much attention to it can last much longer than the emotions that generated the tears. In fact, focusing on a person who is crying will cause that person to be angry with the crisis support team. Team members should simply acknowledge to the group that some aspects of the critical incident are painful and may be hard to discuss. They should reassure the people in the group that intense emotions are very common after tragedies, and that the reactions are expected and healthy. It is also helpful to let the group know that talking about the difficult aspects of a critical incident often helps people to lessen and better control their distressing feelings.

The reaction phase naturally has a great deal of emotional content whether or not crying occurs. Anger, frustration, disappointment, sadness, loss, confusion, and number of other emotions such as guilt and emotional numbness emerge in this phase.

5. Symptoms

*The symptoms phase transitions the group members from the affective domain back into the **cognitive domain**.* Most CISM teams report that this is usually the shortest phase. That observation is accurate. By the time the symptoms phase comes up in a CISD, the participants are growing tired. They tend to offer only one or two symptoms when asked about them. Some of the participants remain quiet during this phase.

The question that initiates this phase is "How has this tragic experience shown up in your life?" or "What cognitive, physical, emotional, or behavioral symptoms have you been dealing with since this event?" If the participants are unusually quiet in this phase, simply ask the participants to raise their hands if they experienced sleeplessness or irritability, or frustration, or anger, or changes in eating or other daily behaviors. The team can point out that, by the show of hands, it is easy to see that several members of the group are reacting in similar ways. The crisis team members must be careful to choose common symptoms that many people have encountered in past events. The CISM team should listen carefully during this phase since they will be using the signs and symptoms of distress presented by the participants in the "Teaching phase."

6. Teaching

The teaching phase is predominantly in the **cognitive domain.** Some of the most important issues addressed by the CISD team in this phase include

- normalizing the symptoms discussed by participants;
- mentioning symptoms that group members did not bring up in the symptoms phase;
- providing information on practical stress management tactics;
- providing explanations for some of the group members' reactions;
- engendering hope of recovery in the participants;
- discussing issues brought up by the participants such as the grief process, suicidal ideation, length of time usually required for recovery;
- discussing steps people may take to recover from the stressful experience;
- addressing any other topic that appears pertinent to the group's needs.

Remember, the teaching phase is the second most important phase in the CISD process. Team members have to be careful to give enough information without over doing it. Too much information is almost as useless and sometimes as painful as insufficient information. With too much information, it is harder for the distressed participants to understand what the presenter is telling them or to make choices regarding their options. A balanced, logical and rational presentation of stress management information is the hallmark of a skillful crisis response team.

7. Re-entry

The reentry phase is definitely a **cognitive domain phase.** The re-entry phase is the time for participants to ask any additional questions that they may have or to make any final statements about the traumatic experience. The CISM team, on the other hand, should be prepared to summarize the CISD and make some final statements. They will be briefly summarizing what has happened in each of the phases of the process. Final explanations, information, action directives, guidance, and thoughts should be presented to the group. Handouts are also distributed. When it is over, the participants should feel that the CISD process itself has reached a conclusion. The loose ends need to be tied up and people should have a sense of what they can do that will be helpful to them. The group members should not feel that there remains substantial unfinished business.[13, 14]

Each of the seven phases has a specific purpose and each phase is linked to the other phases. Always apply the phases in the order given above. The overall strategy in CISD is to move the group from the cognitive domain through the affective domain and back again to the cognitive. Skipping steps disrupts the process and may cause it to fail. Likewise, rushing through the steps is an unwise use of the CISD process and may threaten the effectiveness of the CISD.

► The Five-Phase CISD

There are three circumstances listed below in which the seven-phase process must be altered to accommodate special needs of certain groups or circumstances. Remove the thought phase and the symptoms phase of the standard CISD to formulate a five-phase CISD. We remove the thought and the symptoms phases because they are burdensome or inappropriate under certain circumstances. The five-phase CISD is used:

- On the first day, within hours of **line of duty death** cases. The five phase CISD is applied instead of the defusing process described in chapter ten.

- On the first day, within hours of a **suicide of a colleague**. The five phase CISD is applied instead of the defusing process.

- *Anytime a team is dealing with* **a homogeneous group of children in the six- to twelve-year-old bracket**.

In the first two cases, line-of-duty death and suicide of a colleague, the defusing is simply too weak to be helpful. The emotions in the homogeneous group are already extremely intense. In fact, the intensity of the emotions in suicide and line-of-duty death cases is well beyond that which a defusing can manage. On the other hand, the seven-phase CISD would open up too much emotional content. The middle ground, therefore, is the five–phase CISD as a substitute for the defusing on the day of the death. It "buys" time for the CISM team to organize other interventions, such as the individual support services, the seven-phase CISD and a range of family support services.[13, 14]

When assisting a *homogeneous* group of children in the six- to twelve-year-old age category, the five-phase CISD makes the most sense. Children, after a traumatic event, are distressed and experiencing emotions beyond what a defusing can manage. The defusing does not provide enough support. The seven-phase CISD is far too much for children. It is too long in time and it requires cognitive and affective processes that children of that age have not yet fully developed. The five-phase CISD is, therefore, the very best choice for a homogeneous group of children between six and twelve years of age. It is shorter in duration and goes deep enough into emotional material without overdoing it.

If a crisis team is called upon to assist a group of children 13-years-old or older, the seven-phase CISD process can be used because older children have developed the cognitive and verbal skills that are required in the seven-phase CISD. They have also matured sufficiently to allow a somewhat more affective domain discussion.

SAMPLE PROMPTS for a FIVE-PHASE CISD:

1. Introduction – Five-Phase CISD

- Acknowledge the loss. Offer condolences from the CISM team members.
- This CISD will help us to clarify the group needs, provide helpful information, and guide the group.
- Review the CISD guidelines and start the process.
- With a homogeneous group of 6- to 12-year-old children, acknowledge that an upsetting event has occurred and that crisis team will lead the group through a conversation about the event. Let the children know that by discussing the event we can learn how to deal with it a little better. Make sure that the crisis team uses age appropriate language when working with children.

2. Fact – Five-Phase CISD

- Those who were at the scene of this tragic event will have more information than those who did not.
- "It is helpful for everyone if those who know what happened can tell the group. Please help us if you can."
- When dealing with a homogeneous group of 6- to 12-year olds, let the children know that each can be helpful to their friends by sharing what they know about the experience. In that way, the adults leading the meeting can help to clarify things and can clear up any misunderstandings.

3. Reaction – Five-Phase CISD

- "What is the worst aspect of this terrible event for you right now?"
- "What are you having the most difficult time with now?"
- With 6- to 12-year-old children, the crisis team leaders can ask, "What is hard for you right now?" or "Is there one thing about the situation that bothers you more than anything else?" Then go on to say something such as, "Let's talk about those things and see if we can find some things that might make us feel a little better."

4. Teaching – Five-Phase CISD

- The next few days are going to be very difficult on all of you. We will give you some ideas that might help you as you prepare for the funeral.
- Few details, if any, about the funeral arrangements are likely to have been developed since this loss just occurred.
- Rest when you can.
- Eat. You are stressed and need nourishment.
- Talk to people you trust.
- Prepare for the funeral; assist the person's family and take care of your own family.
- Distress is expected, but it is not easy to deal with.
- Everyone reacts in their own way.
- Here are some common reactions that people encounter after losing a friend or colleague.
- Do not discuss the long-range grief process. They are not ready to hear that yet. Instead, talk about common acute grief reactions.
- **The following pointers are specifically recommended when working with 6- to 12-year-old children in small, homogeneous groups:**
- Be warm, friendly, and kind with children.
- Always use age appropriate language and concepts with children.
- Avoid content that is too difficult to comprehend.
- Avoid discussing material that terrifies children or causes them to become unnecessarily fearful.
- Remain calm and under control as you lead the discussion with the children.

- Thank children when they make a point.

- Praise them for participation.

- Use questions like "Were you sad?" or "Were you mad?"

- Acknowledge, validate, and reassure children as the discussion continues. "You know we are all sad because of what happened." "It is okay to be mad. You know I would have been mad, too, if it happened to me."

- Some children, especially the younger ones, want to hold hands or to be hugged or gently held around their shoulders when they discuss distressing things. Appropriate touch from adults can be reassuring and very helpful to children struggling through the aftermath of a bad occurrence.

- Accept the issues brought up by the children, but make sure that you clarify information so that it is correct and understandable.

- Correct false information or rumors.

- Provide insights that help children put the experience in perspective.

- Let children know that their viewpoints are valuable.

- Discuss the strengths and the things that the children can learn from an upsetting experience.

- Keep information simple.

- Repeat important instructions and guidelines for recovery.

- Keep the information, instructions, and guidelines provided to children positive and upbeat.

- Encourage children to talk to their parents and other trusted adults in their life about the discussion that occurred in the meeting.

- Let children know that they can reconnect to get questions answered or issues clarified by individual contacts right after the meeting or anytime later.

5. Re-entry – Five-Phase CISD

- This loss is shocking and confusing. It brings up many emotions. It is hard to sort through.

- Do you have any questions that we might be able to answer?

- Is there anything we can do to help guide you through the next few days?

- Children (6 to 12 years) need some of the same information, guidance, and reassurance as adults. Be sure to use age appropriate language.
- Let children (6 to 12 years) ask as many questions as they wish.
- With children (6 to 12 years), normalize their experiences and their reactions and keep the information simple and practical.

Special notes on the Five-phase CISD

- The introduction is shorter and begins with an expression of condolences for those who are suffering the loss of a colleague.
- NEVER go around the circle in a line-of-duty death or a suicide of a colleague case.
- Eliminate the thought phase.
- Reaction phase changed to "What is the most difficult aspect of this situation right now?"
- Eliminate the symptom phase
- The main purpose of a five-phase CISD is to assure that all of the participants have the basic information about the loss of their colleague.
- The second goal is to provide guidelines and information for immediate stress management.
- Do not expect a great deal of discussion when working with a group on the day of a line of duty death or the suicide of a colleague. The personnel are likely to be in shock and have not sorted it out sufficiently to engage in discussion.

Special notes on the use of the Five-phase CISD with children

- With children in the six- to twelve-year-old bracket, remember that their attention span is shorter, so a shortened introduction makes sense.
- The main purpose is to lessen the emotional impact of a traumatic event on the children and to help them to cope with their reactions.
- The five-phase CISD with children also helps them to recover as a group so that they can resume their normal activities in the classroom or in the organization to which they belong.
- Discussions with small, homogeneous groups of children do not need to be long in duration. Twenty minutes to a half-hour will generally be sufficient.

- The five-phase CISD helps to normalize reactions and it allows adults to model appropriate behaviors in the aftermath of a traumatic event.

SPECIFICS TOPICS TYPICALLY ADDRESSED IN THE TEACHING PHASE OF A CISD (7-PHASE AND 5-PHASE)

Specific stress management suggestions and guidelines for healthy living are presented throughout the teaching phase. Focal points are:

- Sleep patterns after a distressing experience
- Dreams
- Eating behaviors
- Exercise
- Contact with other people
- Normalcy of stress symptoms
- Explanation of persistent stress symptoms
- Family support
- Child care issues
- Expectations for the future

The CISM team must address, in the teaching phase, any significant issues brought up at any time in the four other segments of the five-phase CISD. The CISM team should address all of the concerns of the participants before the CISD ends.

➤ *Complications*:

The more well-trained the CISM team members are, the less likely they are to encounter complications because they use their knowledge and experience to avoid the problems. When complications do arise, team members can use their knowledge and skills to make adjustments. However, there are complications that are either beyond the control of the team or present special challenges to the team when they arise. They include but are not limited to the following:

- significant resistance from administrative and supervisory personnel;
- excessive delays in notifying a team that a group needs assistance;
- external noise (street noises, sirens, construction sounds) and other distractions that disrupt the CISD;
- extreme temperatures in the room;

- participants who arrive late for the CISD;
- participants who depart from the CISD prematurely;
- inappropriate people showing up for a CISD, such as bystanders who were at the scene, or children of a volunteer fire fighter, or high ranking officials who were not part of the incident;
- news media coming to the location of the CISD seeking a story;
- an intense emotional discharge during a CISD;

►Military Adaptations

The CISD process has been used within American military forces as well as in the military forces of several other nations for approximately twenty years. Little adaptation to the actual model is required. The adaptations in the military have more to do with issues such as targeting the appropriate units for the intervention, timing, and having sufficient numbers of trained people to provide the services.

►Contraindications

The small group CISD process is contra-indicated in the following circumstances:

- when the group is *heterogeneous;*
- with individuals especially anyone who is injured or ill;
- when the mission is incomplete and still in very active stages;
- when personnel are extremely fatigued or emotionally distraught;
- when personnel are not psychologically ready for the CISD;
- with children below the age of six because they lack the verbal skills, intellectual concepts and emotional maturity to participate in the type of discussion required in a CISD.
- when the majority of the group members are openly hostile to one another;
- within hours of the traumatic event when physical and emotional tension is very high.

►Follow-up

Follow-up is **always** necessary after a CISD. Most of it is of an individual nature, but education, family support, and follow-up meetings are also possible. Use phone calls or face-to-face individual contacts to follow-up with the members of a small group.

SUMMARY

The CISD is the most challenging of all the crisis support techniques for small groups. It has, however, been successfully applied for more than 30 years and it remains popular among military and emergency operations personnel, school systems, businesses, industries, churches, and in communities. That, in itself, is a testimony to the power of this special support service for small groups.

REFERENCES - Chapter 11

1. Mitchell, J.T. (2003). Major Misconceptions in Crisis Intervention. *International Journal of Emergency Mental Health*, 5 (4), 185-197.

2. Mitchell, J.T. (2004). Characteristics of Successful Early Intervention Programs. *International Journal of Emergency Mental Health*, 6 (4), 175-184.

3. Everly, G.S., Jr. & Mitchell, J.T. (1999). *Critical Incident Stress* Management: A new era and standard of care in crisis intervention. Ellicott City, MD: Chevron Publishing Corp.

4. Raphael, B. & Wilson, J.P. (2000). Introduction and overview: Key issues in the conceptualization of debriefing. In B. Raphael and J. Wilson (Eds.) *Psychological debriefing: Theory, practice and evidence*. Cambridge, UK: Cambridge University Press, 1-14.

5. Marshall, S.L.A. (1944). *Island Victory*. New York: Penguin Books.

6. Marshall, S.L.A. (1947). *Men Under Fire: The Problem of Battle Command in Future War*. New York: William Morrow.

7. Marshall, S.L.A. (1956). *Pork Chop Hill*. New York: William Morrow & Co.

8. Shalev, A.Y. (1994). Debriefing following traumatic exposure. In R. J. Ursano, B.G. McCaughey & C.S. Fullerton (Eds.) *Individual and Community Responses to Trauma and disaster: The Structure of Human Chaos (pp. 201-219)*. Cambridge, UK: Cambridge University Press.

9. Dyregrov, A. (2003). *Psychological Debriefing: A leader's guide forsmall group crisisintervention*. Ellicott City, MD: Chevron Publishing Corporation.

10. National Organization for Victim Assistance. (2002). *NOVA Basic Training Manual*. Washington, DC: Author.

11. Armstrong, K., O'Callahan, W., & Marmar, C. (1991). Debriefing Red Cross personnel: The multiple stressor debriefing model. *Journal of Traumatic Stress*, 4, 581-593.

12. Koshes, R., Young, S., & Stokes, J. (1995). Debriefing following combat. In Office of the Surgeon General (Eds.) *War Psychiatry* (pp.271-290).

13. Mitchell, J.T. & Everly, G.S., Jr., (2001). *Critical Incident Stress* Debriefing: An operations manual for CISD, Defusing and other *group crisis interventionservices, Third Edition.* Ellicott City, MD: Chevron.

14. Mitchell, J.T. (2006). *Critical Incident Stress Management (CISM): Group Crisis Intervention, 4th Edition.* Ellicott City, MD: International Critical Incident Stress Foundation.

15. Gilmartin, K.M. (2002). *Emotional Survival for Law Enforcement: A Guide for Officers and Their Families.* Tucson, AZ: E-S Press.

16. Chemtob, C. (2000). Delayed debriefing: after a disaster. In B. Raphael and J. Wilson (Eds.) *Psychological debriefing: Theory, practice and evidence.* Cambridge, UK: Cambridge University Press, 227-240.

17. Mitchell, J.T., Schiller, G., Eyler,V.E. and Everly, G.S. Jr. (1999). Community Crisis Intervention: the Coldenham tragedy revisited. *International Journal of Emergency Mental health*, 1, 227-236.

Chapter 12

Measuring the Success of Crisis Support for Groups

"Go to your bosom;
Knock there, and ask your heart what it doth know."
~ 'Measure for Measure', William Shakespeare,
English dramatist & poet (1564 - 1616)

INTRODUCTION

The measurement of the effect of any group process is not a simple and easy task. Numerous factors, such as those thoroughly described in Chapters five and six, can have an influence on the outcome of group interventions, especially when they occur in the midst of crisis reactions among the group members. However, if we take the necessary time and ask the right questions, we can gain useful insights into what does or does not have a positive influence on crisis support procedures for groups.

As was previously pointed out in Chapter four, the preponderance of group intervention research by the most skillful researchers in the group field has consistently demonstrated the positive effects of group interventions. One review of more than 700 studies in the group literature found that all had positive outcomes.[1]

This chapter will bring some sense of balance, clarity, and, perhaps, an appropriate perspective to a confusing, decade-old argument about the effectiveness of debriefing or more specifically, Critical Incident Stress Debriefing (CISD). The literature review in this chapter will cover both sides of the argument. Those who need to pursue a more detailed review of the literature should read the original studies in their entirety. That is the best way to be fully informed.

ESSENTIALS for UNDERSTANDING the ARGUMENT

To understand the fundamental arguments presented for or against the use of 'debriefing,' and particularly the Critical Incident Stress Debriefing, several important issues must be clear. The answers to certain questions will influence a person's position in the argument. These questions help us to determine if the interventions evaluated by the research actually meet the definition of the small group intervention, CISD. The questions also help us to determine if the interventions evaluated in the research studies are truly contained within the field of Critical Incident Stress Management. Here are the three most important questions that should guide us in an appropriate evaluation of the literature. Question number 3 is followed by 8 sub questions that help to define the field of Critical Incident Stress Management and the specific seven-phase CISD group process which is only one of many interventions in the CISM field.

1. What is the objective of a particular study?

If a study's goal is to determine whether or not a CISD can prevent post-partum depression in an *individual,* and it does not, it is inappropriate to blame the CISD since the prevention of post-partum depression in individuals was never an intended outcome of the process. Likewise, suppose researchers used a poorly defined *'debriefing'* process to attempt to prevent Posttraumatic Stress Disorder in an *individual burn victim* or an *individual injured auto accident victim.* If PTSD developed anyway, it is flawed thinking process to conclude that it must be the fault of a CISD. Instead, the loosely defined 'debriefing' process that the researchers selected, or more accurately stated, *altered,* is at fault. Researchers in such studies obviously did **not** truly provide a CISD. In such cases, the application of the intervention is inherently flawed and the researchers are responsible for the failure. They either altered the process or applied it inappropriately to an unintended population. Therefore, researchers must present other explanations for the failure of the 'debriefing' in the conclusion section of their articles. For instance, it is a well-supported fact in the trauma literature that physical injury is among the greatest predictors of PTSD and other consequences of exposure to trauma.

2. Are the researchers carefully following the specific crisis support CISD protocol for small groups?

Whenever researchers alter, abandon, or ignore any part of, or even the entire CISD protocol, they are no longer measuring the same process as described in the literature as accepted CISD protocols. A researcher who takes such liberties cannot claim, therefore, that the study actually evaluated the CISD process. In light of alterations to, or the abandonment of the CISD protocol, the conclusions drawn by the researchers about the CISD process are therefore invalid, irrelevant, and not applicable to the CISD process.

3. Do the interventions being studied in a particular research study actually meet the definition of a CISD process for small, homogeneous groups within the broader CISM field?

There are a number of sub-questions that can help us understand whether or not the intervention described within a particular research study accurately matches the definition of a small group CISD as it is described in the CISM literature. They are:

a. **What is CISM?**

The initials stand for a comprehensive, integrated, systematic, and multi-component program or a blended package of many crisis intervention techniques. "Critical Incident Stress Management" is the name of the program.

b. **What is a debriefing?**

The term, *debriefing* is a loosely defined term that actually has many different meanings. Business, industry, politics, psychosocial services, the space program, the CIA, and the military all utilize debriefings. The dictionary defines a debriefing as a process to interrogate or question to obtain useful information. The American Psychological Association defines *debriefing* in the following manner, "*n.* the process of giving participants in a completed research project a fuller explanation of the study in which they participated than was possible before or during the research." [2, (p. 258)]

c. **Are there different types of debriefing?**

As the above paragraph clearly points out, there are many types of *debriefing.* They do not necessarily mean a crisis support service for groups. In fact, each of the many types of debriefing has its own purposes, protocols, goals, and objectives. One type of debriefing does not necessarily equate to another type of debriefing.

d. **What is a Critical Incident Stress Debriefing (CISD)?**

A Critical Incident Stress Debriefing (CISD) is a specific, seven-phase, crisis support service for small groups. It is only one of the many techniques under the umbrella of a Critical Incident Stress Management program.

e. **What are the primary goals of a CISD?**

There are three primary goals of a CISD. 1.) Mitigate the impact of a traumatic event and reduce the tension experienced by the group members, 2.) Facilitate, by means of information, support, and guidance, the recovery processes among group members, and 3.) Identify individual members of the group who may need additional support or a referral to other services. Once individuals within the group who are in need of additional support are recognized, the crisis team members help facilitate their access to the necessary resources. All other goals are secondary to those stated in this paragraph.

f. **Is a CISD a psychotherapy process?**

No, it is not any form of psychotherapy! In addition, a CISD does not constitute a substitution for any type of psychotherapy. It is a crisis support service for small, homogeneous groups, designed to enhance group cohesion and restore unit performance, which a traumatic event disrupted.

g. **Who are appropriate targets of the CISD process?**

The CISD process is only for small, homogeneous groups who, as a unit, encountered the same traumatic event. One additional important consideration is that the situation the homogeneous group encountered must be complete or well beyond the most acute, chaotic, or threatening stages before applying a CISD.

h. **Are there contraindications for a CISD?**

Indeed! First, do not apply a CISD to heterogeneous groups. Second, never use a CISD with individuals. The most serious contraindication for a CISD is any application with an *individual* who is ill or injured. It is especially inappropriate to attempt to use the CISD small group process on individual primary victims, such as victims of burns, violence, sexual assault, auto accidents, falls, household or industrial accidents, post-partum depression, difficult pregnancies, or dog bites. In summary, if you are not dealing with a small, homogeneous group, which has experienced the exact same traumatic event, and, if that event is on going, then the CISD is **not** the right choice of intervention.

The three primary questions and the eight secondary questions above can function as both an informational backdrop and a set of research evaluation guidelines. The questions can help us determine if the "debriefing studies" that draw negative conclusions are valid in relation to the specific crisis intervention procedure for small groups, known as Critical Incident Stress Debriefing (CISD).

THE NEGATIVE ARGUMENT

Approximately 18 negative outcome studies purport to study the debriefing process. Almost all use the generic word, *debriefing*, and a few make unsubstantiated claims that they researched the specific CISD process. The paragraphs below provide a brief analysis of these studies.

The first negative 'debriefing' article appeared in 1988. The word 'debriefing' is undefined in the study. One individual at a time received the intervention. All the people in the study were property owners who fought a wild land fire that was threatening their homes. They were not, however, trained firefighters. The people with the most negative outcomes suffered property loss, physical injury, or had greater levels of pre-event anxiety.[3] If we use the questions above as guidelines, it is easy to see several major problems with the study that make it *inapplicable to CISD*.

First, the study uses the generic word 'debriefing.' Second, it explores individual reactions to a traumatic event, not the effects of a group intervention. Third, the targets of the study were inappropriate for CISD because they were individual, primary victims severely threatened by the fire. Some of them even experienced property losses, burns, or other injuries. Fourth, an evaluation of the CISD process was not the objective of this study. Instead, the study focused on an evaluation of the causes and progress of Posttraumatic Stress Disorder among victims of a disaster. Fifth, the study seriously violated the standard protocols and procedures for a CISD. In short, this study was not about CISD and, thus, is irrelevant to CISD.

The next study critical of the 'debriefing' process appeared in 1996. The study purported to assess the effectiveness of stress debriefings with disaster welfare workers after an earthquake. Many serious flaws can be found with a quick perusal of the study. The study does not define the word 'debriefing'. There were several types of undefined 'debriefings' used within the study. The authors themselves state, *"However, there was no standardization of debriefing services…"* [4] (p.47) The authors were uncertain as to whether or not the participants actually participated in some form of a 'debriefing.' They state, *"It was assumed that all subjects in this study who reported having been debriefed did in fact receive posttrauma debriefing."* [4] (p.47) The word *assume* should not appear in a research project of this nature. Researchers should be certain whether or not people received an intervention. There are other problems with the study. There was no homogeneous group. The researchers did not use standard CISD protocols. Furthermore, the president of the Critical Incident Stress Management Foundation, Australia, states that "...*neither Mitchell's CISD, nor Dyregrov's PD, had been taught to rescuers or to the mental health professionals who served them at the time of this study. The actual nature of the interventions remains a mystery!"* [5] This research project did not actually study CISD and it is, therefore, irrelevant and inapplicable to it.

In 1998, the Cochrane Review issued an initial report on 'debriefing.' Six randomized control studies were included in the report. All six studies consisted of *individual counseling sessions with medical patients* in medical care facilities.[6] *These six research projects did not include any form of* group *debriefing.* In the simplest of terms, not one of these studies matched the definition of a CISD and none of them evaluated the actual CISD small group process. Therefore, they are unsuitable to evaluate the CISD process and cannot legitimately be applied to it.

Two of the studies, in fact, demonstrated positive results with individuals; two of the studies had neutral results; and the remaining two studies showed negative outcomes with individuals. Based on the balanced outcomes (two positive, two negative, and two neutral), it is difficult to understand how the authors could conclude that 'debriefings,' especially the CISD, should be discontinued. First, as pointed out in the previous paragraph, none of the six studies actually evaluated the CISD process. Second, it would have been equally legitimate for the researchers to conclude that 'debriefings' ought to be continued based on the results of the studies. The most logical conclusion, of course, would have been that no conclusions were possible with the available data and that further study was required. The conclusion drawn by the authors is even more curious since they did not study any form of group debriefing whatsoever. The report, while shedding light on the enormous difficulties encountered when there is no clear definition of the term 'debriefing,' is unsuitable for an evaluation of the small group CISD process.[7]

In 2000, the authors of the Cochrane Review responded to the considerable criticism that followed the publication of the initial report.

They acknowledged that debriefing research had a bias toward individual (1:1) 'debriefings.' *They further noted that the research on 'debriefing' may have not followed standard debriefing practices.* They also noted that they had not adequately or systematically evaluated timing issues in the application of psychological debriefings on individuals. Nor did they take into consideration the nature of the trauma, the facilitators' training and experience, and the nature and quality of the 'debriefing' itself. They did admit that there was a strong argument in favor of providing psychological support during the acute phases of a crisis and that psychological debriefing had value in this regard. They concluded that their calls to discontinue 'debriefings' were premature.[8]

An update of the Cochrane Review appeared in 2002. The review included eleven "Randomized Control Trials" and one unpublished study. These studies were supposed to be the most robust of all the studies on 'debriefing.' Although most of the studies used the word 'debriefing,' not a single study actually explored the small group CISD process. Again, by utilizing the questions elaborated earlier in this chapter, it is easy to identify numerous flaws in the Cochrane Review on 'debriefing.' Not one of the twelve studies followed the procedures for the small group CISD. Two of them actually predated the first course on CISD and did not mention the word 'debriefing' in any context. One glaring comment in the report makes it abundantly clear that there was no evaluation of the small group CISD. The authors state, *"We are unable to comment on the use of group debriefing, nor the use of debriefing after mass traumas."* [9] (p.10)

Table 12.1 provides crucial information about what was and was not studied by the twelve research projects that make up the Cochrane Review issue on 'debriefing.'[10-21]

Remember that the CISD was developed for use with small, homogeneous groups such as firefighters, paramedics, military personnel, law enforcement personnel and other groups that are thought of as if they were a single entity. It was never intended, nor is it currently intended for use with individuals. The following quotes from the very first article on CISD should allay any misconceptions about the intended use of the CISD process.

"...the facilitator...should have a fairly good background in group dynamics or group interactions."
"A good working knowledge...of the operational procedures of the emergency services group are essential for the success of the debriefing." *"...group discussion of the incident"* *"Participants....";*
"members"; "...group"; "...Groups..."[21] (p.38)

Table 12.2 provides a summary, at a glance, of the categories of studies that the Cochrane Review portrays as related to 'debriefing.' This book does not discuss a few, much less robust studies than those discussed in the Cochrane Review. They did not meet the criteria for inclusion in the Cochrane Review and, because they were too weak to be included in the Cochrane Review, they do not add additional information worthy of discussion. Each of those weaker studies evaluated work with individuals who were primary victims of different traumatic events. None of them is applicable to the CISD process since it is not for use on either individuals or primary victims.

Table 12.1

Study Authors	Subjects	Group or Individuals?	Percentage of Cochrane Review's Report on 'debriefing'
All studies	primary victims	Individuals	100%
	Emergency or Military personnel	Homogeneous groups	0%
1. Bisson et al. (1997)	Burn patients	Individuals	8.5%
2. Bordow & Porritt (1979)	Hospital ER patients	Individuals	8.5%
3. Bunn & Clark (1979)	Relatives of ER Patients	Individuals	8.5%
4. Conlon et al. (1999)	Motor vehicle accident victims	Individuals	8.5%
5. Dolan Unpublished Data	Accident victims house fire victims industrial accident victims	Individuals	8.5%
6.. Hobbs et al. (1996)	Auto accident victims	Individuals	8.5%
7. Lavender & Wilenshaw 1998	Birth mothers	Individuals	8.5%
8. Lee et al. (1996)	women who miscarried	Individuals	8.5%
9.Mayou et al. (2000)	Auto accident victims	Individuals	8.5%
10. Rose et al. (1999)	Sexual assault victims	Individuals	8.5%
11. Small et al.	Birth mothers	Individuals	8.5%
12. Stevens & Adshead (Hobbs & Adshead) 1997	Dog bite victims Auto accidents Assault victims	Individuals	8.5%

Table 12.2

An overview of categories of studies in the Cochrane Review purported to be related to 'debriefing'

Category	Percentage of Cochrane Review Report
Individual auto accident victims	25%
Individual emergency Room patients from house fires, falls and other physical traumas	25%
individual burn victims	8.5%
Individual dog bite victims	8.5%
Individual sexual assault victims	8.%
Individual pregnancy problems a. birth mothers b. women who miscarried c. cesarean section d. difficult pregnancies	25%
groups of emergency personnel	0%
groups of military personnel	0%
Homogeneous groups	0%

There are a few other points worth noting. Both the Bisson (1997) and the Hobbs (1996) studies failed to achieve equality of the subjects on the pretest despite efforts at randomization. The study subjects who were in the 'debriefed' category in both studies had more severe injuries and spent more time in the hospital than did the people who were in the 'non-debriefed' category. As a result, randomization failed and these studies may be flawed beyond meaningful interpretation.[22]

In the Bisson study (1997), the authors state that the differences between the subject categories at the first evaluation, before the individual 'debriefing,' were "associated more strongly with poorer outcome as measured at 13 mos. than were [debriefing] status." [10] (p.79) That is, the cause of a negative outcome was more likely to be the more serious burns and the higher stress scores before the individual 'debriefing' than the effects of the 'debriefing.' Strangely, the non-standard 'debriefing' and not the greater severity of injury was blamed for the negative outcomes. Such an apparently biased conclusion, particularly in light of the authors own statement as quoted above, is illogical and is beyond comprehension.

In the Hobbs study (1996) the differences between groups before the individual 'debriefing' took place were substantial. Therefore, attempts at randomization failed. Those designated to receive the individual 'debriefing' had distress scores two times greater than those who were designated not to receive the individual 'debriefing.' The change in the stress assessment scores from first evaluation to post 'debriefing' were *not clinically meaningful, and do not support the conclusion by the authors that the 'debriefing' was harmful. More severe injuries are a far greater predictor of poor psychological outcome than is receiving an individual 'debriefing.'*

The quality of the Cochrane Review has been called into question. In some reviews, the data did not fully support the conclusion. Errors occur; biases emerge. Users should "interpret the reviews cautiously…"[23] (p.830)

There is an issue of greater concern in the negative argument. The main point of the concern is that researchers insist on evaluating the debriefing process in isolation from its context within a comprehensive, integrated, systematic, and multi-component program. They apparently disregard the guiding questions discussed earlier when they are designing research projects. For reasons that remain incomprehensible, some researchers continue to attempt to research the CISD as if it were a form of psychotherapy instead of a crisis support or psychological first aid technique for groups.

THE POSITIVE ARGUMENT

It is highly recommended that studies in the field of Critical Incident Stress Management review a multi-component approach instead of reviewing only one of the techniques within the CISM field. However, some studies have evaluated only one of the CISM techniques, such as the CISD.

It is interesting to note that studies on the application of the specific, small group CISD process to support homogeneous groups of police officers and firefighters were among the first positive studies in the CISM field. The questions presented earlier can also be applied when evaluating positive outcome studies.

A 1991 study evaluated 40 *police officers* who received a CISD within 24 hours of a traumatic incident in comparison to 31 officers without the CISD. Those with the CISD support service for small groups were less depressed, less angry, and had fewer or less severe stress symptoms at three months than their non-debriefed colleagues.[24]

In 1995 the same study design was applied to trauma-exposed *firefighters*. The study evaluated 30 firefighters who received the CISD support service for small groups and compared them to 35 who did not. At three months, anxiety symptoms were lower in the CISD group than in the non-CISD group.[25]

Another early study of the CISD process found that in a sample of 288 *emergency, welfare, and hospital workers*, 96% of emergency personnel and 77% of welfare and hospital employees stated that they had experienced symptom reduction, which was attributed partly to attendance at a CISD.[26]

After a mass shooting in Texas in 1994 in which 23 people were killed and 32 were wounded, *emergency medical personnel* were offered a small group CISD within 24 hours. A total of 36 respondents were involved in this longitudinal assessment of the effectiveness of CISD interventions on homogeneous groups. Recovery from the trauma appeared to be most strongly associated with participation in the CISD process. In repeated measures at eight days, and again at one month, anxiety, depression, and traumatic stress symptoms were significantly lower for those who participated in CISD than for those who did not participate.[27]

Following hurricane Iniki in Hawaii, researchers obtained pre- and post-test comparisons of two groups of *disaster workers* in a carefully thought out, controlled, time-lagged design study. There were 41 total participants in the study. One group was evaluated; they then performed disaster work. They were given a CISD upon completion of their work. The second group was a replacement group for the first group. The researchers evaluated them before they deployed into disaster work. Their first assessment was before work and, of course, prior to receiving a group CISD process. Since the first group of disaster workers already completed their work and the CISD, their post-CISD assessment was obtained concurrently with the pre-CISD assessment of the incoming group. The intervention package comprised of a CISD plus a stress management education session. This study was among the first to evaluate a package of interventions instead of a single intervention. The CISD reduced posttraumatic stress symptoms in both groups.[28]

Some *emergency personnel* who worked during the civil disturbance in Los Angeles in 1992 received a CISD in small homogeneous groups. Others did not receive a CISD. Command staff decided whether or not their personnel needed the service. The personnel had worked at the same events. Those who received CISD scored significantly lower on the Frederick Reaction Index at three months after the CISD compared with those who did not receive it.[29]

In 1994 more than 900 people drowned in the sinking of the ferry, *Estonia*. Three homogeneous groups of *emergency personnel* who received a CISD small group intervention were compared to one homogeneous group of emergency nurses who did not receive a CISD. Symptoms of posttraumatic stress were lower in each of the CISD groups than in the non-CISD group.[30]

Not all positive outcome studies are within emergency services. In a study of a crisis intervention program, a year without a crisis support program for *bank employees* was compared to a year in which a CISM program was available. Employees fared better with the CISM program. Sick leave in the year in which a CISM program was available was 60% lower. Additionally, workers compensation claims were lower by 68%.[31]

A cost-benefit analysis study evaluated a CISM program for *nurses* in rural areas of northern Canada. The study involved 236 nurses (41% of the work force). The administration introduced a CISM program as a means of controlling stress reactions. Sick time utilization, turnover, and disability claims dropped dramatically after the program was in place. The cost benefit analysis showed that $7.09 (a 700% benefit) was saved for every $1.00 spent on building the CISM program.[32]

A recent study evaluated group crisis support for people working in New York City at the time of the World Trade Center attacks on September 11, 2001. *Employees* who were offered crisis intervention services by their employers were compared to other workers whose employers did not offer any form of organized crisis intervention services. Assessments, conducted at one year and again at two years after the traumatic events of September 11, indicate that those who received group Critical Incident Stress Management services demonstrated benefits across a spectrum of outcomes in comparison to workers without crisis intervention services. Lower levels of alcohol dependency, anxiety, PTSD symptoms, and depression were among the outcomes that indicated a marked difference between those who received CISM services and who were not offered such services.[33]

Studies are now demonstrating that CISM services in general, and the CISD process for small groups in particular, are successful stress management tactics for *military personnel*. For example, in a Randomized Control Trial with British military peacekeepers from Bosnia, 32 only received stress information before deployment. An additional 23 other soldiers received the stress information, but they were also provided with a CISD immediately after returning home. Those who received the CISD had lower stress scores at one year. Alcohol use was substantially lower in soldiers who had received the CISD.[34]

Nine *military personnel* participated in a CISD group intervention after they experienced a fatal auto accident. Nine firefighters served as a control group after they too had experienced a fatal auto accident. The researchers used the PTSS-10 assessment tool and found that the scores had declined in the CISD group when follow-up measures were made at two weeks.[35]

In another Randomized Controlled Trial, *homogeneous groups of bank employees* participated in CISD after distressing robberies. Some received the CISD within ten hours of the incident. Other bank employees were given a CISD at 48 hours after the incident. At two weeks post-CISD, the early-CISD stress scores were statistically significantly lower than the later-CISD scores.[36]

Both CISD by itself and CISD within a CISM program have been effective in reducing distress among bank employees who became robbery victims at the work site. The broader CISM program was clearly more effective than the CISD by itself.[37]

Finally, one longitudinal study thoroughly reviewed the effectiveness of a CISM program for *hospital staff* who were assaulted at work in the course of performing their duties. Raymond Flannery's Assaulted Staff Action Program [ASAP;[38] (a CISM program)] was selected by the American Psychiatric Association as one of the 10 best research programs in 1996. A 10-year review of ASAP practice revealed the ASAP CISM to be clinically effective.[39] Recently Flannery presented a 15-year review of the program and again demonstrated clinical effectiveness.[40]

There are many other such studies. A full presentation of the literature would make this chapter burdensome. For additional information on CISM research, please start by reading the reviews already performed on the CISM literature.[7,41-46]

SUMMARY

Professionals and peers have applied elements of psychological first aid characterized by early supportive intervention for more than a hundred years. Systematic crisis intervention programs originated in the military during World War I and spread to emergency services organizations by the mid 1970s. Critical Incident Stress Management (CISM) emerged in the 1970s as a comprehensive approach to delivering an effective, integrated, systematic, and multi-component, emergency support system. Organized crisis support or Critical Incident Stress Management programs later spread to businesses and industries, school systems, churches, and communities.

The evidence presented in this chapter, which covers several decades, indicates that a wide range of organizations, through their crisis support teams, have successfully provided actual crisis and disaster mental health services in the field, not just in a laboratory. After considering relevant research, the American Psychiatric Association's 1989 Task Force on the Treatment of Psychiatric Disorders concluded over a decade ago that crisis intervention offers a "sound approach" and is an "effective model" for assisting people in emotional distress.[47]

The majority of individuals and groups exposed to a traumatic event will rebound by their own natural recovery mechanisms. When a "safety net" is needed for those who have difficulty in the recovery process, early psychological intervention, including crisis support for groups, under the umbrella of the Critical Incident Stress Management program, has proven to be a useful tool. When properly trained providers adhere to standardized protocols and procedures, as demonstrated by the research in this chapter, they may exert enormous positive influence on the people they support.

REFERENCES - Chapter 12

1. Fuhriman, A., & Burlingame, G. M. (1994). *Handbook of group psychotherapy: An empirical and clinical synthesis.* New York: John Wiley & Sons.

2. VandenBos, G., Editor in Chief. (2007). *APA Dictionary of Psychology.*Washington, DC: American Psychological Association.

3. Mcfarlane, A.C. (1988).The Etiology of post-traumatic stress disorders following a natural disaster. *British Journal of Psychiatry*, 152, 116-121.

4. Kenardy, J.A., Webster, R.A., Lewin, T.J., Carr, V.J., Hazell, P.L. and Carter, G.L.(1996). Stress Debriefing and patterns of recovery following a natural disaster. *Journal of Traumatic Stress*, 9, 37-49.

5. Robinson, R. (2002). Personal communication.

6. Wessely, S., Rose, S., & Bisson, J. (1998). A systematic review of brief psychological interventions (debriefing) for the treatment of immediate trauma related symptoms and the prevention of post traumatic stress disorder (Cochrane Review). *Cochrane Library*, Issue 3, Oxford, UK: Update Software.

7. Mitchell, J.T. (2003). *Crisis Intervention and Critical Incident Stress Management: A research summary.* Ellicott City, MD: International Critical Incident Stress Foundation.

8. Bisson, J., McFarlane, A., Rose, S. (2000) *Position paper International Society for Traumatic Stress Studies. PTSD Treatment GuidelinesCommittee.* Chicago, IL: International Society for Traumatic Stress Studies.

9. Rose, S., Bisson, J., & Wessely, S. (2002). Psychological debriefing for preventing post traumatic stress disorder (PTSD). *The Cochrane Library,* Issue 1. Oxford, UK: Update Software.

10. Bisson, J.I., Jenkins, P., Alexander, J., & Bannister, C. (1997). Randomized controlled trial of psychological debriefings for victims of acute burn trauma. *British Journal of Psychiatry,* 171, 78-81.

11. Bordow, S. & Porritt, D. (1979). An experimental evaluation of crisis intervention. *Social Science and Medicine,* 13, 251-256.

12. Bunn, T. & Clarke, A. (1979). Crisis intervention. *British Journal of Medical Psychology,* 52, 191-195.

13. Conlon, L., Fahy, T.J., and Conroy, R. (1999). PTSD in ambulant RTA victims: A randomized controlled trial of debriefing. *Journal of Psychosomatic Research,* 46, 37-44.

14. Hobbs, M., Mayou, R., Harrison, B and Worlock, P. (1996). A randomized controlled trial of psychological debriefings of road traffic accidents. *British Medical Journal,* 313, 1438-1439.

15. Lavender, T. Walkinshaw, S.A. (1998). Can Midwives Reduce Postpartume Psychological Morbidity? A randomized trial. *Birth,* 25 (4): 215-219.

16. Lee, C., Slade, P., and Lygo, V (1996). The influence of psychological debriefing on emotional adaptation in women following early miscarriage. *British Journal of Psychiatry,* 69, 47-58.

17. Mayou, R.A., Ehlers, A. and Hobbs, M. (2000). Psychological debriefing for road Traffic accident victims: Three-year follow up of a randomized controlled trial. *British Journal of Psychiatry,* 176, 589-593.

18. Rose, S. and Bisson, J. (1998). Brief early psychological interventions following trauma: A systematic review of literature. *Journal of Traumatic Stress,* 11, 697-710.

19. Small, R., Lumley, J., Donohue, L., Potter, A. and Waldenstrom, U. (2000). Randomized controlled trial of midwife led debriefing to reduce maternal depression after operative childbirth. *British Medical Journal,* 321, 1043-1047.

20. (Stevens and Adshead) Hobbs G., Adshead, G. (1997). Preventive psychological intervention for road crash victims. In M. Mitchell (Ed.) *The aftermath of Road Accidents: Psychological, Social and Legal Perspectives,* 159-171. London, UK: Routledge.

21. Mitchell, J.T. (1983) When disaster strikes:The critical incident stress debriefing process. *Journal of Emergency Medical Services*, 13(11), 36–39.

22. Campbell, D.T. and Stanley, J.C. (1963*) Experimental and Quasi-experimental Designs for Research.* Chicago: Rand McNally.

23. Olsen, O. et al. (2001, Quality of Cochrane reviews: Assessment of sample from 1998. *British Medical Journal, 323: 829-832.*

24. Bohl, N. (1991). The effectiveness of brief psychological interventions in police officers after critical incidents. In J.T. Reese and J. Horn, and C. Dunning (Eds.) *Critical Incidents in Policing, Revised (pp.31-38).* Washington, DC: Department of Justice.

25. Bohl, N. (1995). Measuring the effectiveness of CISD. *Fire Engineering*, 125-126.

26. Robinson, R.C. & Mitchell, J.T. (1993) Evaluation of psychological debriefings. *Journal of Traumatic Stress*, 6(3), 367-382.

27. Jenkins, S.R. (1996). Social support and debriefing efficacy among emergency medical workers after a mass shooting incident. *Journal of Social Behavior and Personality, 11,* 447-492.

28. Chemtob, C., Tomas, S., Law, W., and Cremniter, D. (1997). Post disaster psychosocial intervention. *American Journal of Psychiatry,* 134, 415-417.

29. Wee, D.F., Mills, D.M. & Koelher, G. (1999). The effects of Critical Incident Stress Debriefing on emergency medical services personnel following the Los Angeles civil disturbance. *International Journal of Emergency Mental Health,* 1, 33-38.

30. Nurmi, L. (1999). The sinking of the Estonia: The effects of Critical Incident Stress Debriefing on Rescuers. *International Journal of Emergency Mental Health,* 1, 23-32.

31. Leeman-Conley, (1990). After a violent robbery. *Criminology Australia,* April /May, 4-6.

32. Western Management Consultants. (1996). *The Medical Services Branch CISM Evaluation Report.* Vancouver, B.C.: Author.

33. Boscarino, J. A., Adams, R.E. and Figley, C.R. (2005). A prospective cohort study of the effectiveness of employer sponsored crisis intervention after a major disaster, 7 (1), *International Journal of Emergency Mental Health, 7(1)* 31-44.

34. Deahl, M., Srinivasan, M., Jones, N., Thomas, J., Neblett, C., & Jolly, A. (2000). Preventing psychological trauma in soldiers. The role of operational stress training and psychological debriefing. *British Journal of Medical Psychology, 73,* 77-85.

35. Eid, J., Johnsen, B. H., & Weisaeth, L. (2001). The effects of group psy-

chological debriefing on acute stress reactions following a traffic accident: a quasi-experimental approach. *International Journal of* Emergency Mental Health, 3, 145-154.

36. Campfield, K. & Hills, A. (2001). Effect of timing of critical Incident Stress Debriefing (CISD) on posttraumatic symptoms. *Journal of Traumatic Stress*, 14, 327-340.

37. Richards, D. (2001). A field study of critical incident stress debriefing versus critical incident stress management. *Journal of Mental Health, 10*, 351-362.

38. Flannery, R.B. (1998). *The Assaulted Staff Action Program: Coping with the Psychological Aftermath of Violence.* Ellicott City, MD: Chevron Publishing.

39. Flannery, R.B., Jr. (2001). Assaulted Staff Action Program (ASAP): Ten years of empirical support for Critical Incident Stress Management (CISM). *International Journal of Emergency Mental Health*, 3, 5-10.

40. Flannery, R.B. (2005). Assaulted Staff Action Program (ASAP): Fifteen years of Empirical Findings. Paper presented at the 8th World Congress on Stress Trauma and Coping: Crisis Intervention: Best Practices in Prevention, Preparedness and Response. Baltimore, Maryland, USA February 16-20.

41. Hiley-Young, B. & Gerrity, E.T. (1994).Critical Incident Stress Debriefing (CISD): Value and limitations in disaster response. *NCP Clinical Quarterly*, 4, 17-19.

42. Dyregrov, A. (1997). The process in critical incident stress debriefings. *Journal of Traumatic Stress, 10, 589-605*

43. Dyregrov, A. (1998). Psychological debriefing: An effective method? *TRAUMATOLOGYe, 4*, (2), Article 1.

44. Everly, G.S., Jr., Flannery, R. B., Jr., Eyler, V. & Mitchell, J.T. (2001). Sufficiency analysis of an integrated multi-component approach to crisis intervention: Critical Incident Stress Management. *Advances in M i n d Body Medicine*, 17, 174-183.

45. Everly, G.S., Flannery, R. and Mitchell, J.T. (2000). Critical Incident Stress Management (CISM): A review of the literature. *Aggression and Violent Behavior: A Review Journal*, 5, 23-40.

46. Mitchell, J.T. (2004b). *Critical Incident Stress Management (CISM): A defense of the field* . Ellicott City, MD: International Critical Incident Stress Foundation.

47. Swanson, W.C., & Carbon, J.B. (1989). Crisis intervention: Theory and Technique. In Task Force Report of the American Psychiatric Association. *Treatments of Psychiatric Disorders*. Wash. D.C.: APA Press.

Index

About the Author

Jeffrey T. Mitchell, Ph.D., CTS, is a Clinical Professor of Emergency Health Services at the University of Maryland in Baltimore County, Maryland, and President Emeritus of the International Critical Incident Stress Foundation. He taught elementary school science for three years. He earned his Ph.D. in Human Development from the University of Maryland.

After serving as a firefighter/paramedic, Dr. Mitchell developed a comprehensive, systematic, integrated, and multi-component crisis intervention program, "Critical Incident Stress Management." He has authored more than 250 articles and 10 books in the stress and crisis intervention fields.

Dr. Mitchell serves as an adjunct faculty member of the Emergency Management Institute of the Federal Emergency Management Agency. He is a reviewer for the Journal of the American Medical Association and the International Journal of Emergency Mental Health. He has been honored by the Austrian Red Cross with the Bronze Medal for his work in Crisis Intervention.

Dr. Mitchell is board certified in traumatic stress and credentialed as a Diplomate and a Member of the Board of Scientific and Professional Advisors of the American Academy of Experts in Traumatic Stress. He has been approved as a Certified Trauma Specialist by the Association of Traumatic Stress Specialists. The United Nations has appointed him as an expert consultant to the United Nations Department of Safety and Security Working Group on Stress.